Flavor of
THE SOUTH

MALLARD PRESS
An imprint of BDD Promotional Book Company, Inc.,
666 Fifth Avenue, New York, N.Y. 10103.

Mallard Press and its accompanying design and logo
are trademarks of BDD Promotional Book Company, Inc.

CLB 2328
© 1989 Colour Library Books Ltd., Godalming, Surrey, England.
Published in the United States of America in 1989 by The Mallard Press.
Printed and bound in Spain by Graficromo, S.A.
ISBN 0 792 45061 2

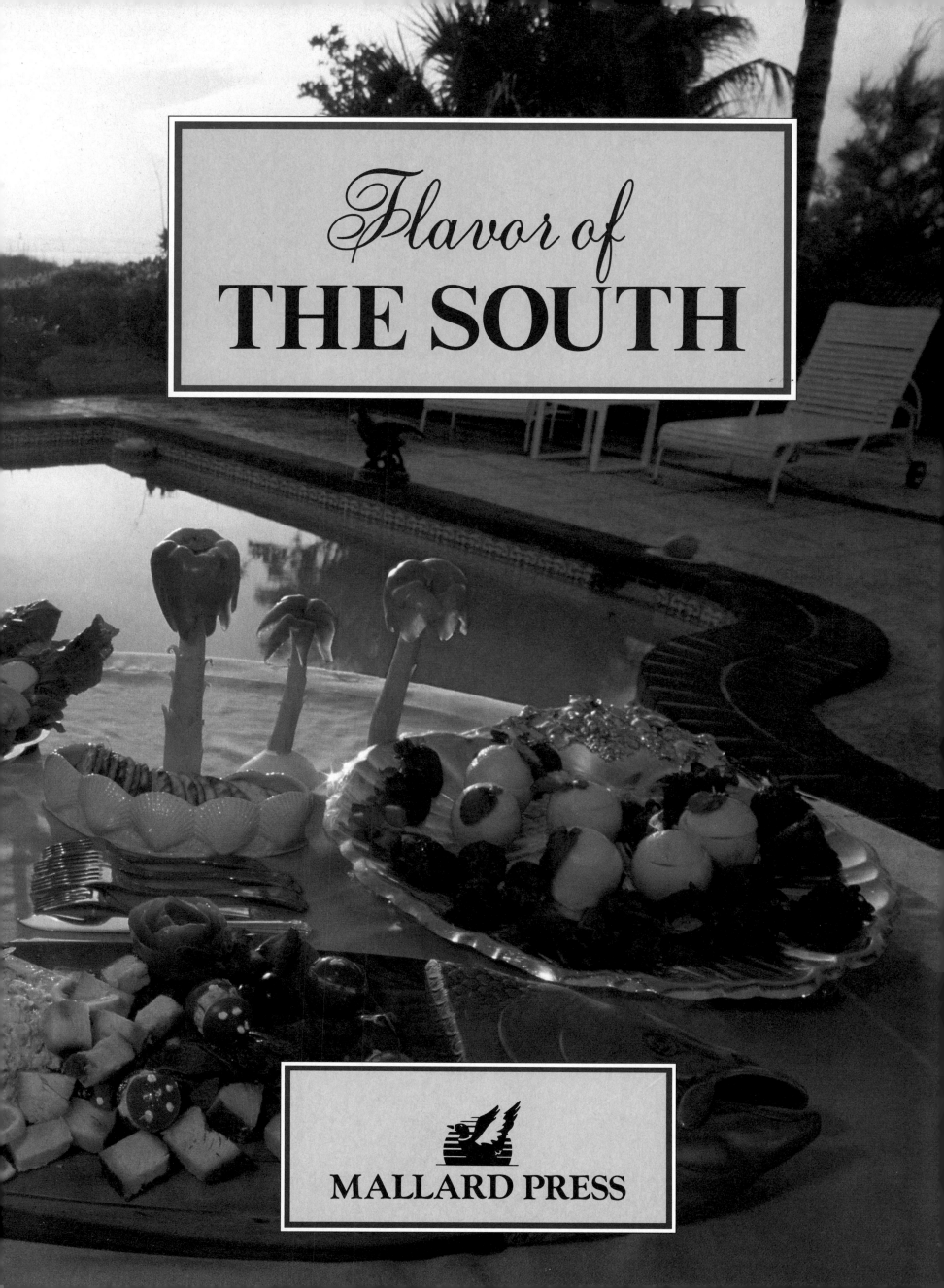

Flavor of
THE SOUTH

MALLARD PRESS

Contents

Introduced by Judith Ferguson
Designed by Sally Strugnell and Alison Jewell
Food Photography by Peter Barry
and Jean-Paul Paireault

Southern hospitality: the words bring to mind warmth, friendliness and gracious living, in all of which food plays an important part. The roots of Southern cooking stretch a long way back into American history and mirror the development of the eleven Southern states themselves.

Florida usually brings to mind beaches with fine, white sand, but the state also boasts history in beautiful old cities like St. Augustine, natural beauty in the mysterious Everglades and a complete change of scene in the rolling hills around Tallahassee. Its Southern heritage is evident in its many seafood recipes, in old-fashioned dishes like Collard Green Soup and in the famous Key Lime Pie.

Georgia has always been famous for its peanuts and peanut soup makes a creamy, velvety first course. Barbecues offer an opportunity to get together and have a feast with friends. For a big celebration, a whole barbecued pig is spectacular and tastes especially good with a spicy Georgia-style sauce.

South Carolina abounds with specialties influenced by the French Huguenot settlers, who helped to colonize the area as early as 1566. Thus Huguenot Torte is a dessert very similar to the French clafoutis, and Halidon Hall Potted Birds owe all their succulence and flavor to a classic French cooking method.

North Carolina has an abundance of dairy products, from which heavenly desserts are made, but the area also provides game, freshwater fish and seafood, which each form the basis of many popular recipes, such as Pan Roasted Quail, Trout in Brown Butter, and Sea Island Shrimp.

Food in Virginia still reflects this state's English background and includes dishes such as Salamagundi, a salad popular in eighteenth century England, and teatime treats such as Maids of Honor.

Some of the loveliest landscapes in the United States are formed by the bluegrass pastures of Kentucky, land of the Derby and of that most famous Southern refreshment, the mint julep. Kentucky was also home to the Shakers, an offshoot of the English Quakers, who prided themselves on using local ingredients in ways that were unpretentious yet tasty and imaginative.

Tennessee was considered the wild frontier of colonial America, so its historical recipes represent basic southern fare. Recipes for cornbread, biscuits, potato salad and, of course, barbecued chicken and ribs are all given here. For dessert you can't beat a fresh fruit cobbler with a light shortcake top.

Alabama provides recipes for those traditional Southern favorites, fried chicken and baked ham, the latter given a new twist with a Cola glaze. On sultry summer days, a cooling salad of butter beans is just the thing to accompany either dish. Desserts like floating islands and charlottes show an early French influence, too.

Mississippi represents what everyone thinks of as the Old South, with its stately mansions, sprawling plantations and the riverboats, which still ply the local waters. Mississippi cooking contains both formal dishes, like Chicken Vicksburg, which are suitable for the most elegant dinner party, and equally delicious but informal ones, like the famous river catfish deep-fried in cornmeal.

From Louisiana come two of the best known American cuisines, Creole and Cajun. The debate about the difference between them will probably go on for ever. Creole cooking centers on New Orleans, whereas Cajun cooking originated in the Louisiana swamps and bayous. Both Creole and Cajun cooking adapted much from classic French cuisine, but the former is said to be more sophisicated and the latter more informal. Both make excellent use of local ingredients and both use a good deal of spices, fresh herbs and peppers, mild and hot. Why not come to your own conclusions by trying out both styles for yourself?

Although definitely part of the South, Arkansas is also a mountain state and the rugged Ozark Mountains have helped to lock in the past and preserve some of the old ways right up to the present day. Food is no exception and Arkansas is home to some real "down home" cooking, like blueberry muffins, peppered ham and okra, a true southern vegetable.

There is a thread of similarity running through all the cuisines of the South, yet they also contain enough variety and individuality to make Southern cooking as fascinating to read about as it is delicious to eat.

Facing page: a breakfast spread at Cedar Grove, Mississippi.

Flavor of **FLORIDA**

COLLARD GREEN
SOUP

These simple ingredients blend together to make a wonderful soup.

PREPARATION TIME: 30 minutes

COOKING TIME: 4 hours

SERVES: 10

INGREDIENTS

- ☐ 2 ham hocks ☐ 2 quarts water
- ☐ 1 cup Great Northern Beans, soaked overnight and drained
- ☐ 1lb Chorizo sausage ☐ 1lb white bacon, diced
- ☐ 1 large onion, chopped ☐ 1 clove garlic, minced
- ☐ 12oz frozen, chopped collard greens ☐ Salt and pepper to taste

Boil the ham hocks in the water for 1 hour. Add the soaked beans to the soup and simmer until tender, about 2 hours. Meanwhile, sauté the sausage, drain and set aside. Clean the frying pan, then sauté the bacon until crisp. Remove and set aside, then fry the garlic and onion in the bacon drippings. When the beans are nearly cooked, add the sautéed bacon, sausage, onion and garlic to the pot. Cook the collard greens in a small amount of boiling water for 15 minutes, or follow the directions on the package. Add to the soup and season to taste with salt and pepper. Simmer for 45 minutes to allow the flavors to blend.

GOVERNOR'S MANSION,
TALLAHASSEE, FL

Previous pages: Cape Florida lighthouse. Above: a layer of cloud intensifies the colors of a sunset over Tarpon Springs. Facing page: Collard Green Soup.

SHRIMP AND MUSHROOM SALAD

This original salad makes use of some of Florida's most delicious seafood.

PREPARATION TIME: 30 minutes

COOKING TIME: 1 minute

SERVES: 8

─────────── I N G R E D I E N T S ───────────

☐ 2lbs cooked shrimp   ☐ ½ lb snow peas, topped and tailed
☐ 1lb very white mushrooms, sliced   ☐ 1 cup toasted pecans
☐ 2 heads Boston or bibb lettuce

─────────── V I N A I G R E T T E ───────────

☐ 1 tbsp Dijon-style mustard   ☐ 1 clove garlic, minced
☐ 4 tbsps cider vinegar   ☐ Dash lime juice
☐ 1 cup salad oil   ☐ Salt and pepper to taste

Peel and devein the shrimp. Blanch the snow peas in the boiling salted water for 45 seconds, then drain. Toss together the mushrooms, shrimp, snow peas and pecans. To prepare the vinaigrette, place the mustard, garlic, lime juice and vinegar in the bowl of a food processor. Pulse a few times, then run continuously while adding the oil in a slow stream. Season with salt and pepper to taste. To serve, toss the salad in the vinaigrette. Line salad plates with the lettuce and arrange the salad on top.

ART SMITH, GOVERNOR'S MANSION,
TALLAHASSEE, FL

Facing page: Shrimp and Mushroom Salad follows the trend towards fresher, lighter food.

FLORIDA SEAFOOD
STEW

This stew makes excellent use of the great variety of Florida's famous seafood. The types of fish and shellfish used can be varied, so make use of the types which are freshest in your area.

PREPARATION TIME: 45 minutes
COOKING TIME: 1 hour 15 minutes (including stock)
SERVES: 8-10

INGREDIENTS
FISH STOCK

- 1 quart cold water   □ 2lbs fish bones and fish heads
- 2 onions, coarsely chopped   □ 2 sprigs parsley, chopped
- 3-4 celery tops, coarsely chopped   □ Juice of ½ lemon
- Salt and freshly ground pepper to taste

STEW

- 1 tbsp butter   □ ⅓ cup olive oil
- 1 tbsp fresh garlic, minced   □ 4 tbsps onion, chopped
- 2 tomatoes, peeled, seeded and chopped   □ 1 tbsp tomato paste
- 1 tbsp fresh parsley, chopped   □ Pinch thyme, saffron and oregano
- Salt and freshly ground pepper to taste
- 2-3lbs fresh fish, boned and cut into chunks
- 2-3lbs shellfish, such as lobster, shrimp, crab, clams or scallops, cleaned, but left in their shells
- 3oz cognac or brandy   □ 1½ cups dry white wine

First prepare the fish stock by combining the fish bones and heads with the water in a large pot. Bring to the boil and add the remaining ingredients. Simmer for 1 hour, skimming as necessary. Strain and set aside. If the stock is made well in advance, keep refrigerated until needed. To prepare the stew, heat the olive oil and butter in a large frying pan. Add the onions, garlic, parsley, tomatoes, tomato paste and seasonings. Sauté for 3-4 minutes, then add the fish and shellfish. Stir and cook for another 1-2 minutes. Pour the cognac over the seafood. Ignite and allow to flame briefly. Transfer the stew to a stew pot, add the white wine and the fish stock. Simmer for another ten minutes before serving.

CHEF HEINZ EBERHARD,
GOURMET GALLEY,
PALM BEACH, FL

Facing page: Florida Seafood Stew.

CLAMS WITH WHITE

WINE SAUCE

PREPARATION TIME: 15 minutes

COOKING TIME: 20 minutes

SERVES: 4

INGREDIENTS

☐ 4 dozen clams, well scrubbed ☐ 1 cup cold water
☐ 2 tsps shallots, chopped ☐ 1 tsp garlic, chopped
☐ 4oz butter ☐ 1 cup dry white wine
☐ Freshly ground pepper to taste ☐ Lemon juice to taste
☐ 2 tsps fresh parsley, chopped

Steam the clams in the water until they open, approximately 5-10 minutes. Discard any that remain closed. Place the clams in a serving bowl and strain and reserve the cooking liquid. Sauté the shallots and garlic in 2oz of the butter for about 5 minutes – do not allow them to brown. Stir in the reserved liquid and the white wine. Bring to the boil and simmer for 5 minutes. Beat in the remaining butter gradually. Do not allow the sauce to boil. Season with freshly ground pepper and lemon juice. Stir in the chopped parsley and pour the sauce over the clams to serve. Serve these delicious clams in bowls, so that guests can savor the rich sauce.

CHEF HEINZ EBERHARD,
GOURMET GALLEY,
PALM BEACH, FL

Above: Clams with White Wine Sauce.
Facing page: the reflective calm of the Florida coastline.

PAELLA

*Florida's Spanish heritage is well reflected in this version
of a classic Spanish dish.*

PREPARATION TIME: 30 minutes

COOKING TIME: 35 minutes

SERVES: 8-10

INGREDIENTS

☐ 2 tbsps olive oil   ☐ 2 tbsps butter
☐ 1 large onion, chopped   ☐ 1 green pepper, chopped
☐ 2 cloves garlic, minced   ☐ 1 chicken, cut into serving pieces
☐ 1lb smoked sausage, cut into 1-inch-thick slices
☐ 12oz yellow rice   ☐ 3 cups stock or water
☐ Salt to taste   ☐ 2lbs shrimp, peeled and deveined
☐ 1lb clams, mussels or lobster (optional)   ☐ 10oz tiny peas

In a paella pan, sauté the onion, green pepper and garlic in a mixture of olive oil and the butter until limp. Remove the vegetables from the pan and set aside. Sauté the chicken pieces and sausage and set aside. Drain the pan, then return the vegetables and meat. Stir in the rice and liquid. Cover the pan with foil and place it in a 350°F oven. Bake for approximately 25 minutes. About ten minutes before the cooking time is up, stir in the seafood and the peas. Continue cooking until the rice is tender and the seafood is cooked but not over done.

GOVERNOR'S MANSION,
TALLAHASSEE, FL

Above: Paella.

FLORIDA LOBSTER

MEDALLIONS

The lobster medallions make a spectacular centerpiece to the Gourmet Galley Raw Bar.

PREPARATION TIME: 45 minutes
COOKING TIME: 10 minutes
SERVES: 4 as an appetizer

―――――― INGREDIENTS ――――――

☐ 1 whole lobster   ☐ ½ lb cream cheese, softened

――――――― GARNISH ―――――――

☐ Black olives, sliced   ☐ Fresh parsley

Place the whole lobster in salted water to cover and bring to the boil. Boil for approximately 5 minutes, or until the lobster turns bright red. Cool, then slit the underside of the tail. Remove the meat, being careful not to cut through the hard top shell. Cut the meat into large, bite-size morsels. Attach the morsels in rows to the top of the lobster shell using the softened cream cheese. Garnish with slices of black olives and parsley.

CHEF HEINZ EBERHARD,
GOURMET GALLEY,
PALM BEACH, FL

Above: the rocky, palm-fringed shore of Conch Key.
Overleaf: Florida Lobster Medallions.

LAKE OKEECHOBEE
CATFISH

PREPARATION TIME: 20 minutes

COOKING TIME: 15-20 minutes

SERVES: 4

INGREDIENTS

- ☐ 4 catfish
- ☐ 1 egg, beaten
- ☐ ¼ cup flour
- ☐ ¾ cup cornmeal
- ☐ 2 tbsps butter
- ☐ 2 tbsps vegetable oil

Clean and skin the fish and remove the heads. Combine the flour and cornmeal. Dip the fish first in the beaten egg and then in the flour mixture until well coated. Heat the butter and oil in a frying pan. Fry the fish, turning once, until they are golden brown.

The cornmeal coating makes this fish extra tasty and crisp. If catfish is not available, why not try this method using another fish. Serve with lemon wedges and tartare sauce.

LIBBY THOMPSON,
GOURMET GALLEY,
PALM BEACH, FL

Facing page: Lake Okeechobee Catfish, a simple tasty dish that's perfect for beach or poolside eating.

WILD DUCK BREASTS WITH RASPBERRIES

PREPARATION TIME: 30 minutes

COOKING TIME: 35 minutes

SERVES: 4

INGREDIENTS

☐ 4 wild duck breasts   ☐ Clarified butter for browning
☐ Salt and pepper to taste

RASPBERRY SAUCE

☐ 1 pint raspberries   ☐ ½ cup water
☐ ½ cup sugar   ☐ 1 cup orange juice
☐ Grated zest of 1 orange

GARNISH

☐ Fresh raspberries   ☐ Fresh mint leaves

First prepare the raspberry sauce by combining the raspberries, water, sugar and orange juice in a saucepan. Simmer the ingredients slowly for 20-25 minutes. Strain the sauce through a fine mesh sieve, then stir in the zest. Set aside while you roast the duck breasts. To prepare the duck, heat some clarified butter in a frying pan and place the duck, skin side down, in the hot pan. Carefully brown the skin. Remove the breasts to a roasting pan and roast on a rack for 10 to 15 minutes. Be careful not to overcook, roast only until the meat is light pink. Towards the end of the cooking time, spoon some of the raspberry sauce over the meat.

To serve, place several spoonfuls of the sauce onto each plate. Slice the meat diagonally and arrange on top of the sauce. Garnish with fresh raspberries and sprigs of mint.

For a very elegant dinner party, accompany this dish with "carved" vegetables. If you don't possess the skill, fresh, lightly cooked vegetables are also good.

GOVERNOR'S MANSION,
TALLAHASSEE, FL

Above: enjoying the last of a beautiful day, promenaders on the pier are silhouetted against the setting sun. Facing page: Wild Duck Breasts with Raspberries.

ROAST LEG OF LAMB

PREPARATION TIME: 15 minutes

COOKING TIME: 1½-2 hours

SERVES: 6-8

──────────── I N G R E D I E N T S ────────────

☐ 1 5-6lb leg of lamb ☐ 6 cloves garlic, crushed
☐ 3-4 tbsps dried rosemary ☐ Salt and pepper to taste
☐ Several sprigs fresh rosemary

Preheat the oven to 450°F. Rub the lamb with salt, pepper, crushed garlic and dried rosemary. Place the meat in a roasting pan and lay sprigs of fresh rosemary on top. Brown the lamb in the hot oven for approximately 15 minutes, or until the meat is sealed, then lower the temperature to 350°F and roast for about 10 minutes per pound (roughly 1¼-1½ hours total).

The rosemary and garlic enhance the delicious flavor of the lamb. The cooking time suggested will produce a medium-rare roast. If you prefer your meat a bit more done, increase the cooking time slightly.

ART SMITH, GOVERNOR'S MANSION,
TALLAHASSEE, FL

Above: garlic and rosemary lend Mediterranean style to Roast Leg of Lamb. Facing page: the County Court House, St. Augustine shows Spanish architectural influences.

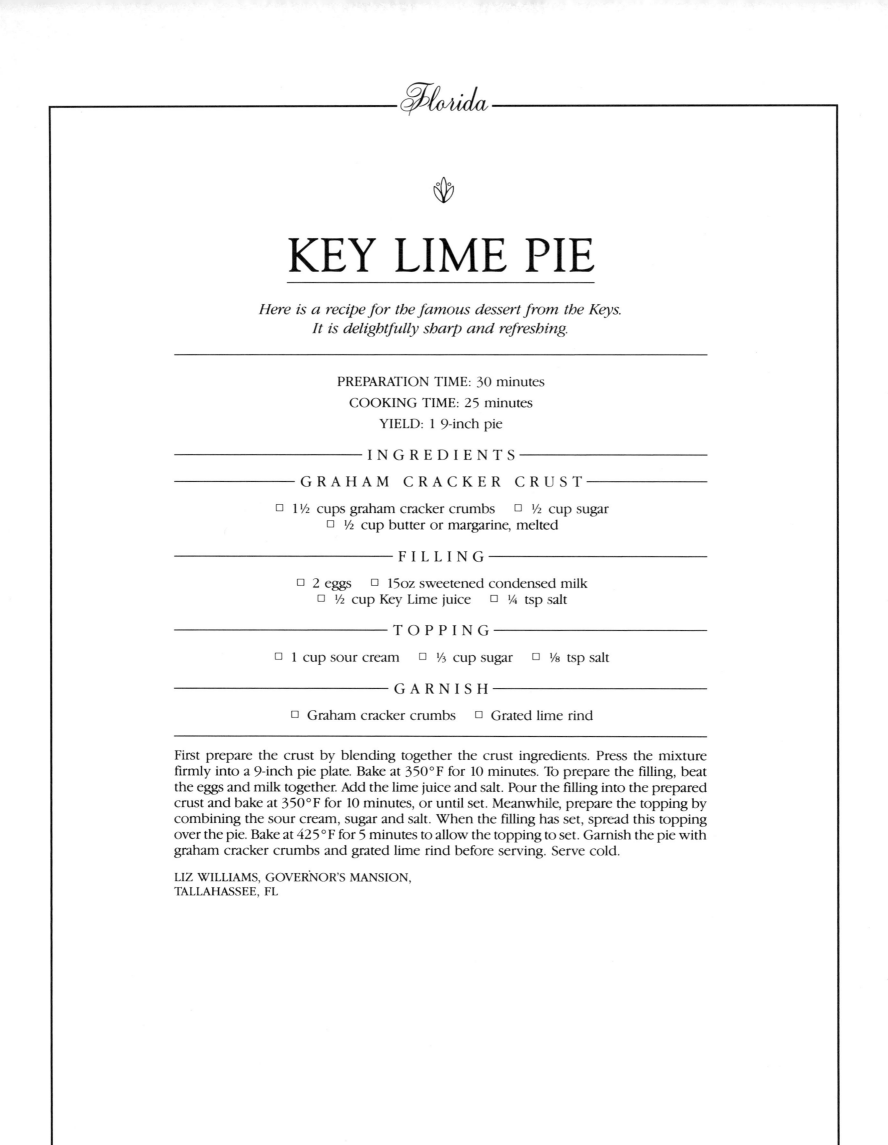

KEY LIME PIE

Here is a recipe for the famous dessert from the Keys.
It is delightfully sharp and refreshing.

PREPARATION TIME: 30 minutes
COOKING TIME: 25 minutes
YIELD: 1 9-inch pie

INGREDIENTS

GRAHAM CRACKER CRUST

☐ 1½ cups graham cracker crumbs   ☐ ½ cup sugar
☐ ½ cup butter or margarine, melted

FILLING

☐ 2 eggs   ☐ 15oz sweetened condensed milk
☐ ½ cup Key Lime juice   ☐ ¼ tsp salt

TOPPING

☐ 1 cup sour cream   ☐ ⅓ cup sugar   ☐ ⅛ tsp salt

GARNISH

☐ Graham cracker crumbs   ☐ Grated lime rind

First prepare the crust by blending together the crust ingredients. Press the mixture firmly into a 9-inch pie plate. Bake at 350°F for 10 minutes. To prepare the filling, beat the eggs and milk together. Add the lime juice and salt. Pour the filling into the prepared crust and bake at 350°F for 10 minutes, or until set. Meanwhile, prepare the topping by combining the sour cream, sugar and salt. When the filling has set, spread this topping over the pie. Bake at 425°F for 5 minutes to allow the topping to set. Garnish the pie with graham cracker crumbs and grated lime rind before serving. Serve cold.

LIZ WILLIAMS, GOVERNOR'S MANSION,
TALLAHASSEE, FL

Facing page: Key Lime Pie, a showpiece dessert for one of Florida's most famous citrus fruits.

FLAN

*Serve this Spanish-inspired dessert with a fruit garnish of
your choice.*

PREPARATION TIME: 20 minutes

COOKING TIME: 45 minutes

SERVES: 6

INGREDIENTS

- ☐ 1 cup plus 3 tbsps sugar ☐ 1 cup milk
- ☐ 1 cup light cream ☐ 4 eggs
- ☐ 4 egg yolks ☐ 1 tsp vanilla
- ☐ Pinch cinnamon, nutmeg and ground cloves

Place one cup of the sugar in a heavy skillet and cook over a high heat, stirring constantly, until the sugar becomes brown and syrupy – it will smoke slightly when it is nearly ready. Use this syrup to coat the bottom and sides of a 6-cup baking dish. Scald the milk and cream. In a separate bowl, whisk together the eggs, yolks, remaining sugar and vanilla. Beat in a little of the hot milk first to stabilize the mixture, then stir in the rest of the hot milk. Strain into the coated baking dish. Place the dish in a pan filled with boiling water and bake at 325°F for 45 minutes, or until a knife inserted in the center comes out clean.

GOVERNOR'S MANSION,
TALLAHASSEE, FL

*Facing page: Flan. Above: Western Lake in Grayton Beach State Recreation
Area is ringed by salt marshes.*

Flavor of
GEORGIA

GEORGIA PEANUT
SOUP

This unusual soup makes delicious use of Georgia's famous peanuts.

PREPARATION TIME: 15 minutes

COOKING TIME: 25 minutes

SERVES: 4-6

INGREDIENTS

☐ 2 tbsps butter ☐ 1 stalk celery, finely chopped
☐ 1 medium onion, finely chopped ☐ 1 tbsp flour
☐ 4 cups chicken stock ☐ ½ cup chunky peanut butter
☐ 1½ cups half and half or milk ☐ Salt and pepper to taste

GARNISH

☐ ¼ cup chopped peanuts ☐ Paprika

In a large saucepan, melt the butter over a low heat. Add the celery and onion and sauté until they are softened but not brown. Stir in the flour to make a smooth paste and cook for 2-3 minutes. Gradually add the chicken stock, stirring to make a smooth sauce. Bring the soup to a boil. Blend in the peanut butter and simmer for about 15 minutes, stirring occasionally. Add the half and half to the pan and heat the soup just to the boiling point. Taste and add salt and pepper if necessary. To serve, garnish each bowl of soup with chopped peanuts and a sprinkling of paprika.

SARALYN LATHAM, THE WILLIS HOUSE,
MILLEDGEVILLE, GA

Previous pages: Georgia's Pioneering territory, near Blue Ridge. Above: Georgia Peanut Soup. Facing page: the stark beauty of Providence Canyon, near Columbus.

JEKYLL ISLAND SHRIMP

Named for an island off the Georgia coast, this makes a rich appetizer or an elegant main course.

PREPARATION TIME: 35-40 minutes

COOKING TIME: 20 minutes

SERVES: 2-4

INGREDIENTS

☐ 2lbs cooked shrimp   ☐ 4 tbsps butter, softened
☐ Pinch salt, white pepper and cayenne   ☐ 1 clove garlic, crushed
☐ 6 tbsps fine dry breadcrumbs   ☐ 2 tbsps chopped parsley
☐ 4 tbsps sherry   ☐ Lemon wedges or slices

To prepare the shrimp, remove the heads and legs first. Peel off the shells, carefully removing the tail shells. Remove the black vein running down the length of the rounded side with a wooden pick. Arrange shrimp in a shallow casserole or individual dishes. Combine the remaining ingredients, except the lemon garnish, mixing well. Spread the mixture to completely cover the shrimp and place in a pre-heated 375°F oven for about 20 minutes, or until the butter melts and the crumbs become crisp. Garnish with lemon wedges or slices.

Above: Jekyll Island Shrimp. Facing page: a Chessar Isle homestead in the Okefenokee swamp area around Folkstone.

COOKING A PIG

If you are planning a really big celebration, you might be interested to know how to cook a pig Georgia style. This method was developed by Bennett Brown's father.

The first point to consider is the pig itself. The ideal pig is one which has been either Federal or State approved, with a dressed (gutted, without head or feet) weight of 110-130lbs. The pig should be split down the breastbone, or butterflied, but not cut in two. Trim away any excess fat in the pig's inner cavity, then liberally salt the entire cavity. This will help to control bacteria and add flavor.

The best way to cook the pig is in a barbecue pit. An easy and inexpensive pit to build is one made of cinder blocks. The pit should be four feet long, four feet wide and three feet deep, with a hole at one end big enough for a shovel to pass through. Make a cooking rack or grill out of metal, preferably stainless steel. The pit may be covered with a piece of plywood.

About ⅓ of a cord of seasoned hardwood, such as oak, hickory, pecan or mesquite, will be needed for the fire which will produce the coals needed for the cooking. Be sure to build the fire in such a way that the coals will be easy to reach through the hole with a shovel.

Build the fire well in advance and prime the pit by heating the grill for 15 minutes. This is similar to preheating an oven and will also kill any bacteria present on the grill. Place the pig on the grill, rib side down. Arrange the coals under the two hams and two shoulders, which are the thickest parts of the pig. It is important to keep a good heat (250-350°F) under the pig at all times, so add new hot coals approximately every 30 minutes. Be careful not to burn the underside of the meat.

The pig should be ready to turn after 10 or more hours, depending on size. After turning, the pig needs constant attention. The heat of the coals will make the back fat liquify and accumulate in the middle rib area. This must be ladled away and discarded, but be careful, the fat is very flammable. During the last three hours, baste the pig with a good barbecue sauce to keep the meat from drying out. When most of the back fat has been rendered, which will take about 5 hours, the pig should be fully cooked. The pig should be cooked enough so that the meat falls off the bone. The pig will serve about 120 people.

BENNETT A BROWN III,
LOWCOUNTRY BARBEQUE CATERING,
ATLANTA, GA

Facing page: a whole barbecued pig will feed family and friends in generous style.
Overleaf: Lowcountry Barbecue Sauce.

4. Stir in sherry. Return stuffed chicken wings and cook only to heat through.

VARIATION: In step 2, stuff wing cavities with a half-and-half mixture of slivered ham and bamboo shoots.

RED-COOKED OR SOY CHICKEN I

4 to 6 servings

1 spring chicken

1 cup soy sauce

water to cover

1. Wipe chicken with a damp cloth. Place in a heavy pan with soy sauce and cold water. Bring to a boil over medium heat; then simmer, covered, until done (30 to 45 minutes). Turn once or twice for even coloring.

2. Let chicken cool slightly. With a cleaver, chop, bones and all, in 2-inch sections; or carve Western-style. Serve hot with its sauce; or serve cold, reserving sauce for later use as a master sauce. (See page 739.)

NOTE: Simmer a 4- to 5-pound bird about an hour.

RED-COOKED OR SOY CHICKEN II

4 to 6 servings

1 cup sherry

½ cup brown sugar

1 cup water

½ cup soy sauce

1 spring chicken

1. Cut scallion stalks in ½-inch sections. Place in a large heavy pan, along with brown sugar, soy sauce, sherry and water. Bring to a boil over medium heat.

2. Wipe chicken with a damp cloth and add to pan. Bring to a boil again; then simmer, covered, 45 minutes, turning bird once or twice for even coloring.

3. Let chicken cool slightly. With a cleaver, chop, bones and all, in 2-inch sections; or carve Western-style. Serve hot with its sauce; or serve cold, reserving sauce for later use as a master sauce. (See page 739.)

NOTE: For a 4- to 5-pound bird, cook 30 minutes on each side, basting frequently.

VARIATION: In step 1, for the scallions, substitute 2 slices fresh ginger root, 1 garlic clove, crushed, and 1 clove star anise.

RED-COOKED OR SOY CHICKEN III

4 to 6 servings

1 spring chicken

1 scallion stalk

½ inch fresh ginger root

2 slices fresh ginger root

½ cup soy sauce

2 tablespoons sesame oil

ipe chicken with a damp cloth. Mince ginger root; then combine with
sherry, salt and pepper. Rub mixture over chicken inside and out. Let
ur.

ut scallion stalk in ½-inch sections. Slice and crush remaining ginger

at oil. Add scallion and ginger root; stir-fry a few times. Add remaining
and bring to a boil. Cook 2 minutes over medium heat.

old chicken upside down over a bowl. Pour heated soy mixture into its
ing it drain out through the neck into the bowl. Repeat 5 times, reheating
r the second and fourth time.

ansfer sauce to a large pan and slowly bring to a boil. Add chicken and
ng, until evenly colored (about 10 minutes).

il water and add to chicken and sauce. Simmer, covered, 10 to 15
Add sugar and simmer, covered, 2 minutes more.

LOWCOUNTRY BARBECUE SAUCE

A spicy sauce, similar to this one, is one of the Brown family secrets.

PREPARATION TIME: 15 minutes

COOKING TIME: 25 minutes

YIELD: approximately 1 quart

INGREDIENTS

- □ 1 quart apple cider vinegar
- □ 1 pint ketchup
- □ ½ tbsp Worcestershire sauce
- □ 2 tbsps black pepper
- □ ¼ tsp cayenne pepper
- □ ½ tbsp salt
- □ 1 tbsp sugar

Boil the vinegar for approximately 10 minutes, then stir in the ketchup and Worcestershire sauce. Reduce the heat to medium and mix in the black and red pepper, salt and sugar. Simmer over a low heat for 15 minutes, stirring often.

BENNETT A BROWN III,
LOWCOUNTRY BARBEQUE CATERING,
ATLANTA, GA

Facing page: Lapham-Patterson House is a carefully restored Victorian showpiece in Thomasville, South Georgia.

CHICKEN AND DUMPLINGS

Chicken and Dumplings brings all the warmth and friendliness of a Georgia country kitchen home to you.

PREPARATION TIME: 20 minutes
COOKING TIME: 2½-3½ hours
SERVES: 6-8

INGREDIENTS

☐ 1 large boiling hen   ☐ 4oz butter
☐ Water to cover   ☐ Salt and pepper to taste

DUMPLINGS

☐ 4 cups plain flour   ☐ 1½ cups ice water

GARNISH

☐ Fresh or dried parsley

Place the hen and the butter in a large pot and pour over water to cover. Boil for 2-3 hours, or until the hen is very tender, adding extra water if necessary. Remove the hen and allow to cool, reserving the broth. When the hen is cool enough to handle, remove the bones, cut the meat into serving-size pieces and return to the broth. To prepare the dumplings, make a well in the middle of the flour. Pour in the ice water and blend with a fork or with your fingers until the dough forms a ball. Roll out thinly and cut into 2-3-inch-wide strips. Bring the chicken and broth to the boil and season to taste with salt and pepper. Slowly drop the dough strips into the broth. Simmer for 2-4 minutes, or until the dumplings are tender. Serve immediately, garnished with dried or fresh parsley.

SARALYN LATHAM, THE WILLIS HOUSE,
MILLEDGEVILLE, GA

Facing page: Chicken and Dumplings. Above: the County Courthouse in Chatsworth is a fine example of Greek Revival architecture.

CHICKEN AND SEAFOOD ROLL-UPS

*These are delicious served with a mushroom cream sauce
for a special occasion.*

PREPARATION TIME: 30 minutes

COOKING TIME: 20-25 minutes

SERVES: 8

INGREDIENTS

☐ 8 chicken breasts, boned   ☐ 2 cups stuffing, such as seasoned bread or corn
bread crumbs, moistened with stock
☐ 1 cup shrimp, cooked and sliced in half   ☐ 8oz crab meat
☐ 1 cup flour, seasoned with salt and pepper   ☐ 4 eggs, beaten
☐ 1 cup milk   ☐ 12oz butter

Combine the stuffing, shrimp and crab meat. Spoon this mixture over the chicken breasts. Roll up the chicken, tucking the ends inside. Dip the rolls first in the beaten eggs, then in flour, then in the milk, then in flour again. Melt the butter in a skillet until bubbling. Gently brown the roll-ups, then drain and place them in an oiled baking pan. Bake at 350°F for 20-25 minutes.

SARALYN LATHAM, THE WILLIS HOUSE,
MILLEDGEVILLE, GA

*Above: the tamed formality of private gardens contrasts with the state's more
rugged natural beauty. Facing page: Chicken and Seafood Roll-Ups.*

CORN BREAD

PREPARATION TIME: 15 minutes

COOKING TIME: 20 minutes

YIELD: 1 9×9 inch bread

INGREDIENTS

□ 2 cups self-rising cornmeal or
2 cups cornmeal plus 3 tsps baking powder
□ 3 tbsps flour   □ 1 tbsp sugar
□ ¼ cup + 2 tbsps vegetable oil   □ 1¾ cups buttermilk
□ 1 egg   □ 3-4 tbsps bacon drippings

Combine all the ingredients except for the bacon drippings and blend well. Bake in a preheated, greased 9×9 inch pan for 20 minutes at 425°F. Spoon the bacon drippings on top, return to the oven and bake until brown. The addition of bacon drippings adds a delicious new twist to an old Southern favorite.

SARALYN LATHAM, THE WILLIS HOUSE,
MILLEDGEVILLE, GA

BISCUITS

These biscuits taste best if served fresh from the oven. This recipe makes enough biscuits to serve the Confederate Army! If you are dealing with a smaller crowd, try using quarter quantities.

PREPARATION TIME: 30 minutes
COOKING TIME: 15 minutes
YIELD: 150

——————————— I N G R E D I E N T S ———————————

☐ 2 ½ lbs self-rising flour   ☐ 1lb shortening
☐ 1 quart buttermilk

Gently blend together all of the ingredients. Roll out on a lightly floured board and cut with a biscuit cutter. Bake on well greased baking sheets at 425°F for 15 minutes, or until golden brown.

SARALYN LATHAM, THE WILLIS HOUSE,
MILLEDGEVILLE, GA

Facing page: placid cattle emphasize the tranquillity of this pastoral scene.
Above: Biscuits.

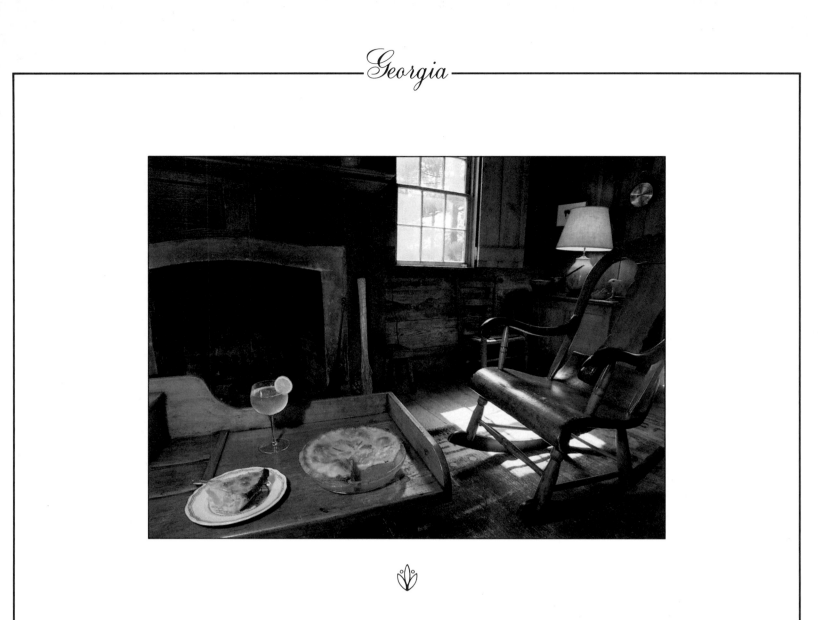

GEORGIA PEACH

PIE

Georgia is famous for its peaches, and this peach pie may be one of the reasons.

PREPARATION TIME: 30 minutes

COOKING TIME: 50 minutes

YIELD: 1 9-inch pie

INGREDIENTS

☐ 1 unbaked 9-inch pie shell, plus pastry top
☐ 4 cups fresh peaches, washed, peeled and sliced
☐ 3 egg yolks   ☐ 3 tbsps flour
☐ 1 cup sugar   ☐ ½ cup butter, melted

Preheat the oven to 400°F. Place the prepared peaches in the pie shell. Blend the egg yolks, flour, sugar and melted butter in a bowl. Pour this mixture evenly over the peaches. Cover with the pastry top and seal around the edges. Cut several slits to allow the steam to escape. Bake for 50 minutes, or until the pastry is golden brown.

ANN DORSEY, FULL SERVICE CATERING,
ATLANTA, GA

Facing page and above: whether you take them with you on a fishing trip or cook them in a pie, Georgian peaches make perfect summer eating.

GEORGIA PECAN CAKE

This makes a delicious and spectacular dessert centerpiece.

PREPARATION TIME: 45 minutes

COOKING TIME: 35 minutes

YIELD: 1 3-layer 9-inch cake

——— INGREDIENTS ———

- ½ cup margarine
- ½ cup shortening
- 2 ¼ cups sugar
- 5 eggs, separated
- 2 ½ cups plain flour
- 1 tsp soda
- 1 cup buttermilk
- 2 tbsps vanilla
- ½ cup grated coconut
- 2 cups pecans, chopped

——— ICING ———

- ½ cup margarine
- 16oz cream cheese
- 2lbs confectioners' sugar
- 3 tbsps vanilla
- ¾ cup pecans, chopped

Using an electric mixer, cream together the margarine, shortening and sugar for 15 minutes on medium speed. Add the egg yolks and continue to mix on low for 5 minutes. Sift the flour and soda together 3 times and add to the mixing bowl alternately with the buttermilk, beginning and ending with the flour. Turn off the mixer and fold in the vanilla, coconut and pecans. Beat the egg whites until stiff, and gently fold in the cake batter. Divide the mixture into 3 greased and floured 9-inch cake pans. Bake at 350°F for 30-35 minutes, or until the cake springs back when touched lightly in the center. Cool for 15 minutes on a rack before turning the layers out of the pans and leaving to cool completely. While the cakes are cooling, prepare the icing. Cream together all of the icing ingredients, except for the pecans. When the cakes are completely cool, spread the icing thickly on top of each cake and sprinkle ¼ cup of the chopped pecans on top. Place the cakes on top of each other to make a three layered cake.

SARALYN LATHAM, THE WILLIS HOUSE,
MILLEDGEVILLE, GA

Facing page: this rich Pecan Cake is a truly Georgia-ous confection!

SYRUP CHIFFON PIE

*Light and creamy, with a wonderful maple and nut flavor,
this is a heavenly dessert.*

PREPARATION TIME: 30 minutes, plus 2 or more hours chilling
COOKING TIME: 7 minutes
YIELD: 1 9-inch pie

INGREDIENTS

CRUST

☐ 1½ cups graham cracker crumbs   ☐ 3oz margarine, melted

FILLING

☐ 1 tbsp plain gelatin   ☐ 5 tbsps cold water
☐ 8oz pure maple syrup   ☐ 3 egg yolks, lightly beaten
☐ Pinch salt   ☐ 1 tsp vanilla extract
☐ 3 egg whites, beaten   ☐ 3 tbsps sugar

TOPPING

☐ 8oz whipping cream   ☐ 1½ cups chopped pecans

To prepare the crust, combine the graham cracker crumbs and melted margarine. Press the mixture over the bottom and sides of a 9-inch pie dish. Bake at 350°F for 7 minutes. Set aside to cool while you prepare the filling.

Soak the gelatin in the cold water and set aside. Combine the maple syrup, egg yolks and salt in the top of a double boiler. Cook slowly over hot water until thick. Stir in the gelatin and the vanilla and mix well. Transfer the mixture to a bowl surrounded by crushed ice. Refrigerate until the custard begins to jell, approximately 20-30 minutes. When the custard is beginning to set, beat the egg whites to soft peaks and gradually beat in the sugar. Gently fold into the custard. Spoon the filling into the prepared crust. Prepare the topping by whipping the cream and folding in the pecans. Spread this topping over the custard. Refrigerate the pie for at least an hour before serving, or until the filling is set.

SARALYN LATHAM, THE WILLIS HOUSE,
MILLEDGEVILLE, GA

*Above: Syrup Chiffon Pie. Facing page: a breeze ripples the surface of a lake in
the Laura S. Walker State Park.*

SHE-CRAB SOUP

*The She-Crab is preferred for this soup because the eggs add a special flavor.
If you are unable to obtain female crabs, crumble the yolk of hard-boiled
eggs into the bottom of the soup plates before serving.*

PREPARATION TIME: 30 minutes

COOKING TIME: 20 minutes

SERVES: 4-6

INGREDIENTS

☐ 1 tbsp butter   ☐ 1 tsp flour
☐ 1 quart milk   ☐ 2 cups white crab meat and crab eggs
☐ ½ tsp Worcestershire sauce   ☐ ⅛ tsp mace
☐ Few drops onion juice   ☐ ½ tsp salt
☐ ⅛ tsp pepper

TO SERVE

☐ 4 tbsps dry sherry, warmed   ☐ ¼ pint cream, whipped
☐ Paprika or finely chopped parsley

In the top of a double boiler, melt the butter and blend in the flour until smooth. Add the milk gradually, stirring constantly. Add the crab meat and eggs and all of the seasonings. Cook the soup slowly for 20 minutes over hot water. To serve, place one tablespoon of warmed sherry in individual soup bowls. Add the soup and top with whipped cream. Sprinkle with paprika or finely chopped parsley.

MRS. HENRY F. CHURCH, CHARLESTON, SC
(FROM "CHARLESTON RECEIPTS,"
COMPILED AND EDITED BY THE JUNIOR
LEAGUE OF CHARLESTON, INC.)

*Previous pages: South Carolina's "Table" mountain. Facing page: She-Crab Soup.
Above: the lights of Pier 14 are reflected in the stillness of the ocean at Myrtle Beach.*

MRS. SAMUEL G. STONEY'S BLACK RIVER PÂTÉ

This is an old French Huguenot dish which has been in the Stoney family for generations.

PREPARATION TIME: 45 minutes

COOKING TIME: approximately 1 hour

INGREDIENTS

- ☐ 3 parts leftover venison
- ☐ 1 part butter
- ☐ Coarse black pepper and salt to taste

Put the venison through the finest blade of a meat grinder twice. Work the pepper into the butter and add salt to taste. Combine the venison and seasoned butter in a Pyrex dish and pound with a wooden mallet until the pâté forms a solid mass. Smooth the top and bake at 325°F for approximately 1 hour, or until golden brown. Chill before serving.

To serve, cut into thin slices and serve with hominy or salad. The pâté will keep indefinitely in the refrigerator.

MRS. WILLIAM S. POPHAM (NEE STONEY)
CHARLESTON, SC
(FROM "CHARLESTON RECEIPTS,"
COMPILED AND EDITED BY THE JUNIOR
LEAGUE OF CHARLESTON, INC.)

Previous pages: Mrs. Samuel G. Stoney's Black River Pâté. Above: the Adventure, *a replica of a 17th-century trading ketch, is moored at Charles Towne Landing.*

MEETING STREET
CRAB MEAT

This tasty seafood dish may also be made with shrimp. Use 1½ lbs raw, peeled shrimp in place of the crab meat.

PREPARATION TIME: 20 minutes

COOKING TIME: 15 minutes

SERVES: 4

INGREDIENTS

□ 4 tbsps butter   □ 4 tbsps flour
□ 1 cup cream   □ 4 tbsps sherry
□ Salt and pepper to taste   □ 1 lb white crab meat
□ ¾ cup grated sharp cheese

In a saucepan, melt the butter. Gradually stir in the flour to make a smooth paste. Cook for a few minutes over a low heat then gradually stir in the cream. Add the sherry, salt and pepper. Cook over a medium heat, stirring often, until the sauce is thickened. Remove from the heat and stir in the crab meat. Pour the mixture into a buttered casserole, or into 4 individual baking dishes. Sprinkle with the grated cheese and bake at 400°F for approximately 10 minutes, or until the cheese melts. Be careful not to overcook.

MRS. THOMAS A. HUGUENIN,
CHARLESTON, SC
(FROM "CHARLESTON RECEIPTS,"
COMPILED AND EDITED BY THE JUNIOR
LEAGUE OF CHARLESTON, INC.)

Above: Meeting Street Crab Meat.

POMPANO À LA GHERARDI

This delicious fish dish is an original creation which was named for Admiral Gherardi.

PREPARATION TIME: 45 minutes
COOKING TIME: 30 minutes
SERVES: 6

INGREDIENTS

□ 6 small pompano   □ Salt and pepper

STUFFING

□ 1lb cooked shrimp   □ ½lb white crab meat

□ ½ loaf bread   □ ½ bunch green onions
□ ¼ cup sherry   □ ½ cup butter
□ 3 tbsps parsley   □ 1 egg

──────────────── GARNISH ────────────────

□ ½ lb cooked shrimp   □ 6 strips bacon
□ ½ cup chopped olives

Remove the heads of the fish and split down the flat side, removing the backbone and ribs to form a pocket. Sprinkle salt and pepper inside and set aside while you prepare the stuffing.

To prepare the stuffing, mince together the shrimp, crab meat, bread, green onions, parsley and butter. Stir in the sherry and egg and season to taste with salt and pepper. Cook over a low heat, stirring frequently until heated through, about 10-15 minutes. Use this stuffing to stuff the fish. Top the pocket opening with the garnish of whole cooked shrimp, chopped olives and strips of bacon. Arrange in a covered casserole and bake at 350°F for 15 minutes, or until the fish is fully cooked.

WALTER L. SHAFFER,
HENRY'S RESTAURANT, CHARLESTON, SC
(FROM "CHARLESTON RECEIPTS,"
COMPILED AND EDITED BY THE JUNIOR
LEAGUE OF CHARLESTON, INC.)

Facing page: Pompano à la Gherardi. Above: Hampton Plantation is one of South Carolina's classic antebellum plantation houses.

LOW COUNTRY OYSTERS WITH MUSHROOMS

*Serve these creamy oysters from a chafing dish
with triangles of hot buttered toast.*

PREPARATION TIME: 30 minutes

COOKING TIME: 15 minutes

SERVES: 8

--- INGREDIENTS ---

☐ 1lb fresh mushrooms, sliced   ☐ 8oz canned pimentos, sliced
☐ 8 tbsps butter   ☐ 8 tbsps flour
☐ 4 cups cream   ☐ 1½ quarts oysters, cleaned
☐ Salt and pepper to taste

Sauté the mushrooms and pimentos in the butter. After the mushrooms have softened, sift the flour over the pan and stir in. When the sauce begins to thicken, add the cream, salt and pepper. In a separate pan, let the oysters simmer in their own liquor until the edges curl. Add the oysters to the mushroom sauce, stirring in additional cream if the dish seems too dry.

MRS. THOMAS A. HUGUENIN,
CHARLESTON, SC
(FROM "CHARLESTON RECEIPTS,"
COMPILED AND EDITED BY THE JUNIOR
LEAGUE OF CHARLESTON, INC.)

*Facing page: "Table" mountain takes its name from an Indian legend, in which a
giant chieftain was said to have dined at its summit.
Above: Low Country Oysters with Mushrooms.*

HALIDON HILL POTTED BIRDS

PREPARATION TIME: 30 minutes

COOKING TIME: 2-3 hours

SERVES: 6

INGREDIENTS

- □ 6 Cornish game hens
- □ Salt and pepper to taste
- □ ½ cup flour
- □ 2½ tbsps lard
- □ Water for cooking

STUFFING

- □ 6 slices toasted stale bread, broken into small pieces
- □ ¼ small onion, minced
- □ 4 slices breakfast bacon
- □ ¾ cup hot water
- □ Salt and pepper to taste

Begin by preparing the stuffing. Fry the bacon until crisp and break up into small pieces. Add the onion and cook until golden, then stir in the bread, salt, pepper and hot water. Mix well.

Wipe the birds inside and out with a damp cloth, then fill lightly with the stuffing. Sprinkle the birds with the salt, pepper and flour. Melt the lard in a cast iron pot or skillet. Brown the birds, then add a little water and cover tightly. Cook very slowly until tender, 45 minutes – 1 hour or more. Add more water if necessary.

The tasty stuffing could also be used to stuff a roast chicken or other larger bird.

MRS. THOMAS A. HUGUENIN,
CHARLESTON, SC
(FROM "CHARLESTON RECEIPTS,"
COMPILED AND EDITED BY THE JUNIOR
LEAGUE OF CHARLESTON, INC.)

Facing page: Greenville's Independence Day celebrations include a hot air balloon competition. Above: Halidon Hill Potted Birds.

FRANCIS MARION RECEPTION PUNCH

This non-alcoholic punch is named after the teetotaller Francis Marion, the revolutionary hero also known as the "Swamp Fox". However, this punch can also be used as the basis for an alcoholic punch by substituting 4 quarts of your favorite alcoholic beverage for the pineapple juice.

PREPARATION TIME: 15 minutes

SERVES: 100

INGREDIENTS

☐ 1 quart frozen orange juice   ☐ 3 quarts ice water
☐ Juice of 18 lemons or 6oz frozen lemon juice   ☐ 4 quarts pineapple juice
☐ 4 quarts carbonated water or ginger ale

Prepare the "stock" by combining the orange juice, ice water, lemon juice and pineapple juice. Mix thoroughly and chill. To serve, pour half of the stock into a large punch bowl and add two quarts of the carbonated water or ginger ale. Use the rest of the stock and carbonated water as needed to keep the punch "alive". The punch may be sweetened with sugar dissolved in water, if desired.

MRS. KATHERINE HERMAN,
CHARLESTON, SC
(FROM "CHARLESTON RECEIPTS,"
COMPILED AND EDITED BY THE JUNIOR
LEAGUE OF CHARLESTON, INC.)

COLONEL AIKEN
SIMONS' MINT JULEP

There are many ways to make a mint julep. Here is the formula as devised by Colonel Aiken Simons, and well loved by his descendants.

PREPARATION TIME: approximately 15 minutes

Take a pitcher or jug of suitable size and add a teaspoon of sugar for each julep. Add just enough water to dissolve the sugar, about an equal volume of water to sugar is sufficient, if you stir well. Pour in a whiskey glass of bourbon for each julep and stir well. Select 4 or 5 fine sprigs of mint and add them to the mixture. Whether this mint should be crushed or not is a subject of great controversy. It depends on the strength of the mint and the taste of the drinkers. Allow to stand for a while.

To serve, fill each glass with broken ice, taking care not to get the outside of the glass wet. Divide the contents of the pitcher among the glasses and stir each vigorously. Fill up the glasses with more ice and stir again briskly. A thick, white coating of frost should have formed on the glass by now. Handle the glass very carefully to avoid marring the frost, because this is the pride and joy of the julep. Choose very fine sprigs of mint for the garnish; place one in each glass and serve.

ALBERT SIMONS, CHARLESTON, SC

Facing page: Francis Marion Reception Punch. Above: the serene beauty of Lake Keowee. Overleaf: Colonel Aiken Simons' Mint Julep.

HUGUENOT TORTE

*Apples and nuts are a delicious addition to this
old-fashioned dessert.*

PREPARATION TIME: 20 minutes

COOKING TIME: 45 minutes

SERVES: 8

INGREDIENTS

□ 2 eggs   □ 1½ cups sugar
□ 4 tbsps flour   □ 2½ cups baking powder
□ ¼ tsp salt   □ 1 cup tart cooking apples, chopped
□ 1 cup chopped pecans or walnuts   □ 1 tsp vanilla

TO SERVE

□ Whipped cream   □ Chopped nuts

Beat the eggs with an electric or rotary mixer until they are very frothy and lemon-colored. Add the remaining ingredients in the order given. Pour the batter into a well-buttered 8 x 12-inch baking pan. Bake at 325°F for about 45 minutes, or until brown and crusty.

To serve, scoop up portions with a pancake turner, keeping the crusty top uppermost. Cover each serving with whipped cream and a sprinkling of chopped nuts.

MRS. CORNELIUS HUGUENIN, CHARLESTON, SC
(FROM "CHARLESTON RECEIPTS,"
COMPILED AND EDITED
BY THE JUNIOR LEAGUE OF CHARLESTON, INC.)

*Above: Huguenot Torte. Facing Page: Cypress Gardens are a 160-acre
wonderland of trees and flowering plants situated north of Charleston.*

LADY BALTIMORE CAKE

*This glamorous cake was made famous in Charleston's
Lady Baltimore Tea Room.*

PREPARATION TIME: 30 minutes

COOKING TIME: 30 minutes

YIELD: 1 large cake

INGREDIENTS

- □ 1 cup butter   □ 3 cups sugar
- □ 4 eggs   □ 1 cup milk
- □ 3½ cups cake flour   □ 4 tsps baking powder
- □ 2 tsps vanilla   □ 2 tsps almond extract
- □ ½ cup water

FROSTING

- □ 2 cups sugar   □ ⅔ cup water
- □ 2 tsps corn syrup   □ 2 egg whites, beaten stiffly
- □ 2 cups seedless raisins, finely chopped and soaked
  overnight in sherry or brandy, if desired
- □ 2 cups pecans or walnuts, finely chopped
- □ 12 figs, finely chopped and soaked overnight in sherry or brandy, if desired
- □ Almond and vanilla extract, to taste

Using an electric mixer, cream the butter. Add 2 cups of the sugar gradually and beat to the consistency of whipped cream. Add the eggs one at a time and beat thoroughly. Sift together the baking powder and flour three times. Add alternately with the milk, using a wooden spoon to blend. Pour the batter into two greased 11-inch cake pans and bake at 350°F for 30 minutes, or until done. While the cakes are baking, make a thick syrup of the remaining cup of sugar and the water. Flavor with the almond and vanilla extract. When the cake is baked, cool in the pans for 10 minutes, then turn the layers out onto a rack for complete cooling. As soon as you remove the layers from the pans, spread the prepared syrup on top.

To prepare the frosting, combine the sugar, water and syrup in a saucepan. Cook until the mixture forms a firm ball when a spoonful is dropped into cold water. Pour this syrup gradually into the stiffly beaten egg whites, beating constantly. Add the raisins, nuts and figs. Finally stir in the almond and vanilla extracts to taste. When the cake is cool, spread this frosting between the layers and on the top and sides of the cake.

MRS. HOWARD READ, CHARLESTON, SC
(FROM "CHARLESTON RECEIPTS,"
COMPILED AND EDITED BY THE JUNIOR
LEAGUE OF CHARLESTON, INC.)

*Facing page: Lady Baltimore Cake reflects the elegance for which the town of
Charleston is famous.*

Flavor of
NORTH CAROLINA

TROUT IN BROWN BUTTER WITH PECANS AND MINT

Browned butter with lemon, pecans and mint is used to complement crispy fried fresh trout – a winning combination.

PREPARATION TIME: 20 minutes

COOKING TIME: approximately 30 minutes

SERVES: 4

─────── I N G R E D I E N T S ───────

- 4 whole rainbow trout, 8-10oz each
- 2 cups milk
- ½ cup fresh lemon juice
- 1 cup all-purpose flour
- ½ cup stone-ground yellow cornmeal
- 2 tbsp Kosher salt
- 1 tsp black pepper, coarsely ground
- ½ tsp paprika

Previous pages: the Blue Ridge Mountains south of Asheville. Above: Trout in Brown Butter with Pecans and Mint. Facing page: hens roam freely outside an old wooden homestead.

BROWN BUTTER SAUCE

☐ ½ lb butter, softened   ☐ 1½ cups pecans, coarsely chopped
☐ ¼ cup lemon juice   ☐ ¼ cup spearmint leaves, chopped

TO FRY

☐ Peanut oil

GARNISH

☐ Mint sprigs   ☐ Lemon crowns

To cook the trout, first rinse them under cold water, then soak them, refrigerated, for 2 hours in a mixture of the milk and the lemon juice. Meanwhile, combine the flour, cornmeal, salt, pepper and paprika. Remove the trout from the marinade, drain and roll them in the seasoned flour mixture. It is easiest to cook the trout in two batches. Heat a small amount of peanut oil in a large skillet over a high heat until it is nearly smoking. Carefully place two of the trout in the pan and reduce the heat to medium high. Cook for 4 minutes before turning, then reduce the heat to medium. Cook for a further 3-4 minutes, or until the trout tests done at the backbone. Cook the remaining trout in the same way. When cooked, arrange the fish on individual plates or on a large platter.

To prepare the Brown Butter Sauce, melt the softened butter in an 8-inch skillet over a high heat. Add the pecans and cook until the butter begins to darken and the nuts start to brown. When the butter ceases to foam and clarifies, carefully add ¼ cup lemon juice and the chopped mint leaves. Pour the sauce over the cooked trout and garnish with a lemon crown and a mint sprig.

BEN BARKER, FEARRINGTON HOUSE,
CHAPEL HILL, NC

SEA ISLAND SHRIMP

*Although this is a recipe from the Carolinas, it is popular
everywhere succulent shrimp are available.*

PREPARATION TIME: 30 minutes

COOKING TIME: 15 minutes

SERVES: 2-4

INGREDIENTS

□ 2 dozen raw large shrimp, unpeeled   □ 4 tbsps butter or margarine
□ 1 small red pepper, seeded and finely chopped
□ 2 green onions, finely chopped
□ ½ tsp dry mustard   □ 2 tsps dry sherry
□ 1 tsp Worcestershire sauce   □ 4oz cooked crab meat
□ 6 tbsps fresh breadcrumbs   □ 1 tbsp chopped parsley
□ 2 tbsps mayonnaise   □ Salt and pepper
□ 1 small egg, beaten   □ Grated Parmesan cheese   □ Paprika

Remove all of the shrimp shells except for the very tail ends. Remove the black veins on
the rounded sides. Cut the shrimp down the length of the curved side and press each
one open. Melt half of the butter or margarine in a small pan and cook the pepper to soften,
about 3 minutes. Add the green onions and cook a further 2 minutes. Combine the peppers
with the mustard, sherry, Worcestershire sauce, crab meat, breadcrumbs, parsley and
mayonnaise. Add seasoning and enough egg to bind together. Spoon the stuffing onto
the shrimp and sprinkle with the Parmesan cheese and paprika. Melt the remaining butter
or margarine and drizzle over the shrimp. Bake in a pre-heated 350°F oven for about 10
minutes. Serve immediately.

Above: Sea Island Shrimp.
Facing page: a weatherboarded shoemaker's shop in Old Salem.

PAN-FRIED
PORK CHOPS

The cornmeal coating makes these pork chops crisp and tasty!

PREPARATION TIME: 15 minutes
COOKING TIME: approximately 15 minutes
SERVES: 4

INGREDIENTS

□ 4 8oz center cut pork loin chops   □ ½ cup all-purpose flour
□ ¼ cup stone-ground cornmeal   □ ½ tsp salt
□ ¼ tsp black pepper, ground   □ ⅛ tsp cayenne pepper
□ ⅛ tsp paprika   □ Peanut oil for cooking

Combine the flour, cornmeal and spices and dredge the pork chops in this seasoned mixture until they are coated. Heat a cast-iron or other heavy-bottomed frying pan over a medium high heat for 3 minutes, then brush the pan with a thin film of peanut oil. When the oil just smokes, add the coated pork chops and reduce the heat to medium. Cook for 4 minutes, then turn the chops. Cover the pan and cook for a further 4 to 5 minutes, or until the meat is juicy, but no longer pink at the bone.

BEN BARKER, FEARRINGTON HOUSE,
CHAPEL HILL, NC

Facing page: the golden glow of a North Carolinian sunset. Above: Pan-Fried Pork Chops.

PAN-ROASTED QUAIL WITH BLACK-EYED PEAS, VINAIGRETTE AND FRIED CORNMEAL MUSH

If quail are not available, Cornish game hens (one per person) could be prepared in a similar way.

PREPARATION TIME: 30 minutes
COOKING TIME: 15-20 minutes
SERVES: 4

INGREDIENTS

□ 8 dressed quail, 4½-6oz each

MARINADE

□ ¼ cup molasses   □ ¼ cup bourbon whiskey
□ ½ cup cold-pressed peanut oil   □ 1 tsp salt
□ 2 tbsp fresh tarragon, chopped   □ 2 shallots, finely minced
□ 2 cloves garlic, pressed   □ 6 grinds of fresh black pepper

PAN GRAVY

□ 1 shallot, finely minced   □ 1 clove garlic, finely minced
□ ¾ cup rich chicken stock   □ 1 tsp fresh tarragon, chopped
□ Salt to taste   □ Black pepper to taste

GARNISH

□ Thyme flowers

Rinse the quail and pat dry. Combine the marinade ingredients and marinade the quail for at least 6 hours. Remove the quail from the marinade and pat dry before cooking. Heat a small amount of peanut oil in a large skillet until it is nearly smoking. Add the quail and brown on both sides over a medium-high heat. Reduce the heat to medium, turn the quail breast side up, and cook, covered, for 5-7 minutes, or until the birds are medium-rare. Keep warm in a slow oven while you prepare the pan gravy.

Previous pages: only the guests are missing from this sumptuous Southern dinner of Crab Cakes, Pan-Roasted Quail with Fried Okra and Strawberry Raspberry Shortcakes.

To make the gravy, pour off all of the fat from the pan in which the quail were cooked. Add the minced garlic and shallot and sauté over a high heat until they are lightly browned. Carefully add the bourbon and ignite. When the flames die down, scrape the bottom of the pan. Add the chicken stock, bring the gravy to the boil and cook until reduced by half. Add the chopped tarragon, then adjust the seasoning with salt and pepper.

To serve the quail, make nests of Black-eyed Peas Vinaigrette on beds of curly endive, escarole or other leafy green vegetable on 4 plates. Place triangles of Fried Cornmeal Mush around the edges of the nests and arrange 2 quail on top of each. Pour pan gravy over the quail and garnish with thyme flowers.

BEN BARKER, FEARRINGTON HOUSE, CHAPEL HILL, NC

BLACK-EYED PEAS
VINAIGRETTE

These delicious black-eyed peas were developed to serve with pan roasted quail, but they are too good to restrict to that use. Why not try serving them with other poultry dishes?

PREPARATION TIME: 25 minutes

COOKING TIME: 20-30 minutes

SERVES: 4-6

INGREDIENTS

- ¼ lb bacon, cut into ¼-inch strips
- 3oz onions, coarsely chopped
- 2oz green bell pepper, coarsely chopped
- 2oz celery, coarsely chopped
- 3 cloves garlic, finely chopped
- ½ tsp cayenne pepper
- ½ tsp black pepper
- ¼ tsp white pepper
- ¼ tsp ground cumin
- ½ tsp dried basil
- ¼ tsp dried oregano
- 1 bay leaf
- ¾ lb fresh black-eyed peas, shelled or 1 12oz package frozen black-eyed peas
- 1½ quarts chicken stock, or more if needed
- Salt to taste

VINAIGRETTE

- ¼ cup cider vinegar
- ¼ cup olive oil
- 4 scallions, chopped
- ¼ cup flat-leafed parsley, chopped

Fry the bacon in a large skillet until crisp. Remove the bacon and set aside. Cook the onion, pepper and celery in the bacon fat over a medium heat until they are softened. Increase the heat, add the garlic, herbs and spices and stir and cook for 1 minute. Stir in the black-eyed peas with ¾ quart of stock and bring to the boil. Reduce the heat and simmer the peas until they are tender but firm, adding more stock as needed. When the peas are cooked the liquid should be nearly absorbed. Transfer the black-eyed peas to a large bowl and keep warm. Meanwhile, prepare the vinaigrette by combining the vinegar, oil, scallions and parsley. Toss the peas in the vinaigrette, stir in the reserved bacon, season to taste with salt and allow to cool to room temperature before serving.

BEN BARKER, FEARRINGTON HOUSE,
CHAPEL HILL, NC

WALTER'S FRIED OKRA

This makes a delicious first course, or try serving with meat.

PREPARATION TIME: 15 minutes

COOKING TIME: 15-20 minutes

SERVES: 6-8

INGREDIENTS

- ☐ 1lb fresh okra, washed and trimmed
- ☐ 2 cups buttermilk
- ☐ 1½ cups stone-ground yellow cornmeal
- ☐ ½ tsp cayenne pepper
- ☐ ¼ tsp black pepper
- ☐ ⅛ tsp white pepper
- ☐ ½ tsp salt
- ☐ ⅛ tsp paprika
- ☐ ⅛ tsp ground cumin

TO FRY

- ☐ 4 cups peanut oil

TO SERVE

- ☐ Lemon wedges

Soak the okra in the buttermilk. Meanwhile, combine the cornmeal and the spices. Remove the okra from the buttermilk and roll it in the spiced cornmeal until well coated. Heat the peanut oil in a heavy-bottomed pan to 350°F. Fry the coated okra in batches to a deep golden brown. Drain each batch on absorbent paper and keep warm in a low oven. Serve the fried okra hot with lemon wedges.

WALTER ROYAL, FEARRINGTON HOUSE, CHAPEL HILL, NC

FRIED CORNMEAL
MUSH

Serve this with pan-roasted quail, or to accompany other chicken dishes.

PREPARATION TIME: 15 minutes

COOKING TIME: 10-15 minutes

SERVES: 4-6

INGREDIENTS

☐ 1 quart chicken stock or water   ☐ 1 cup yellow stone-ground cornmeal
☐ 2 tbsps grated Parmesan cheese   ☐ 2 tbsps chives, minced
☐ 1 tsp salt

TO FRY

☐ 2 tbsps flour   ☐ ¼ cup clarified butter

Bring 3 cups of the liquid to the boil. Mix the cornmeal with the remaining cup of liquid and pour this mixture into the boiling liquid, stirring well. Continue to cook until a spoon will stand up in the mush. Stir in the Parmesan cheese, chives and salt. Spread the cornmeal mush over a buttered cookie sheet to a ½-inch thickness. Cool completely, then cut into triangles. Dust the triangles with flour and sauté them in clarified butter until they are golden brown on both sides.

ADAPTED FROM MADELEINE KAMMAN'S
"IN MADELEINE'S KITCHEN" BY FEARRINGTON HOUSE, CHAPEL HILL, NC

*Facing page: an abandoned farmhouse. Above: Fontana Lake is man-made,
the waters contained by the tallest dam east of the Rockies.*

CRAB CAKES WITH RED PEPPER AND TOMATO SAUCE

very good
4/7/05 B.

The addition of peppers and herbs makes these crab cakes especially tasty.

PREPARATION TIME: 15 minutes

COOKING TIME: 10-15 minutes

SERVES: 4 as an appetizer

INGREDIENTS

- □ 1lb crab meat, picked over for shell particles
- □ 2 tbsps red bell pepper, finely chopped
- □ 2 tbsps yellow bell pepper, finely chopped
- □ 2 tbsps green bell pepper, finely chopped
- □ 2 tbsps celery, finely chopped   □ 1 green onion, minced

☐ 2 eggs   ☐ ¼ cup dried bread crumbs
☐ 1 tbsp fresh lemon thyme, chopped   ☐ 1 tbsp flat leaf parsley, chopped
☐ 1½ tsps coarse salt   ☐ ¼ tsp fresh ground pepper
☐ Zest of one lemon, grated

─── TO COOK ───

☐ Clarified butter

─── TO SERVE ───

☐ Sprigs of lemon thyme   ☐ Corn kernels

Combine all the ingredients, except for the lemon thyme sprigs and the corn kernels, in a large bowl and mix well. Form the mixture into cakes 1½ inches in diameter and ½ inch thick. Sauté in clarified butter over medium heat for approximately one minute on each side, or until the cakes are lightly browned.

To serve, place a spoonful of Red Pepper and Tomato Sauce on each plate. Arrange several crab cakes on top and garnish with sprigs of lemon thyme and kernels of corn.

BEN BARKER, FEARRINGTON HOUSE, CHAPEL HILL, NC

RED PEPPER AND TOMATO SAUCE

Serve this flavorful sauce with crab cakes or other seafood.

PREPARATION TIME: 20 minutes

COOKING TIME: 10-15 minutes

SERVES: 4

─── INGREDIENTS ───

☐ 4 plum tomatoes, peeled, seeded and coarsely chopped
☐ 3 red bell peppers, roasted, peeled, seeded and coarsely chopped
☐ 1 tbsp tomato paste   ☐ 3 tbsps lemon thyme, chopped
☐ Salt to taste   ☐ Pepper to taste
☐ Tabasco sauce to taste   ☐ Lemon juice to taste

─── GARNISH ───

☐ 1 ear Silver Queen corn, or other white variety,
shucked and removed from the cob

Combine the tomatoes and peppers in a heavy-bottomed saucepan. Simmer over medium-low heat until they are very soft. Purée in a food processor, or pass through the fine blade of a food mill. Stir in the tomato paste and leave to cool. When cool, add the lemon thyme and season with salt, pepper, Tabasco sauce and lemon juice to taste. Garnish the sauce with corn kernels which have been blanched in boiling salted water for 15 seconds, then drained and refreshed in cold water.

BEN BARKER, FEARRINGTON HOUSE,
CHAPEL HILL, NC

Facing page: Crab Cakes with Red Pepper and Tomato Sauce.

STRAWBERRY RASPBERRY SHORTCAKES

Strawberries and raspberries make a rich and delicious combination in this elegant shortcake recipe.

PREPARATION TIME: 30 minutes
COOKING TIME: 10-12 minutes
SERVES: 8

INGREDIENTS

SHORTCAKES

- 3 cups all-purpose flour
- 1½ tbsps baking powder
- ¾ tsp salt
- ¼ cup plus 2 tbsps sugar
- Zest of 1 orange, finely grated
- 1 tbsps orange juice
- 7 tbsps butter at room temperature, cut into small pieces
- ½ cup milk
- 6 tbsps heavy cream

FILLING

- 1 pint fresh strawberries, sliced
- 1 pint fresh raspberries
- Sugar to taste

Combine the flour, baking powder, salt, sugar, orange zest and juice in a mixing bowl. Cut in the butter, then add the milk and cream and stir lightly until the mixture forms a dough which is thick but not sticky. Roll out the dough to a ½-inch thickness on a lightly floured surface. Cut into 3 ½-inch rounds with a biscuit cutter and place on a parchment-lined baking sheet. Bake at 375°F for 10–12 minutes, or until the tops are golden brown.

To prepare the filling, combine the strawberries and raspberries, sprinkle on sugar to taste and leave to stand for several hours to allow the juices to be drawn out. To assemble, cut each shortcake in half, lightly butter and toast. Cool slightly, then soak the shortcake halves in the collected berry liquid. Place 8 of the halves on plates, cover each with a large spoonful of the berry mixture, allowing some of the berries to cascade onto the plate. Cover with the remaining shortcake halves.

KAREN BARKER, FEARRINGTON HOUSE,
CHAPEL HILL, NC

Facing page: azaleas grow well in North Carolina and always provide a splash of bright color.

CHOCOLATE MINT TORTE WITH BOURBON CRÈME ANGLAISE

This rich and elegant torte makes the perfect ending to a very special meal.

PREPARATION TIME: 1½ hours
COOKING TIME: approximately 2 hours
SERVES: 12

INGREDIENTS

TORTE

- ☐ 10oz semi-sweet chocolate   ☐ 5oz unsalted butter
- ☐ 7 eggs, separated   ☐ 1 cup sugar
- ☐ ⅓ cup white crème de menthe liqueur   ☐ 1 tsp pure mint extract
- ☐ ¼ tsp salt

GANACHE TOPPING

- ☐ ½ cup heavy cream   ☐ 4oz semi-sweet chocolate, cut into small pieces

CRÈME ANGLAISE

- ☐ 2 cups light cream or 2 cups half and half
  or 1 cup heavy cream + 1 cup milk
- ☐ 7 egg yolks   ☐ ¾ cup sugar
- ☐ 3 tbsps bourbon

To prepare the torte, melt the chocolate and butter in a double boiler, then set aside to cool slightly. In a large bowl, beat the egg yolks with ¾ cup of the sugar until very thick and light. Add the cooled chocolate mixture, the crème de menthe and the mint extract and stir until just mixed. In a separate bowl beat the egg whites with the remaining ¼ cup of sugar and the salt until they form soft peaks. Quickly, but gently, fold the egg whites into the chocolate mixture. Pour the batter into a buttered and floured 10-inch spring-form pan, the bottom of which has been lined with parchment paper. Bake at 300°F for 1 hour, followed by 30 minutes at 250°F. Remove the cake from the oven and immediately run a sharp knife around the sides of the pan to prevent the top of the cake from cracking. Place the pan on a wire rack and allow the torte to cool completely before removing the sides of the pan.

While the torte is cooling, prepare the ganache topping. Heat the cream in a small, heavy-bottomed saucepan over a low heat. Add the chocolate pieces and stir constantly until the chocolate is completely melted. Remove the pan from the heat and place it in an ice bath. Cool, stirring constantly, until the mixture is thickened, but still spreadable. Spread the ganache evenly over the top of the cooled cake. Chill the torte briefly to set the topping.

To prepare the Bourbon Crème Anglaise, beat the egg yolks with ½ cup of the sugar until thick and light. Heat the light cream with ¼ cup of the sugar. Add a little bit of the hot cream to the egg yolks to prevent them from curdling, then gradually add the yolk mixture to the hot cream in the saucepan. Cook over low heat, stirring constantly until the mixture thickens and coats the back of a spoon. Add the bourbon, then strain the Crème Anglaise into a storage container. Chill in the refrigerator until needed.

To serve the torte, cut with a thin-bladed knife which has been warmed, and clean the knife between each cut. Serve the torte at room temperature with the chilled Bourbon Crème Anglaise.

TORTE RECIPE ADAPTED FROM
MAIDA HEATLER "BOOK OF GREAT CHOCOLATE DESSERTS" BY FEARRINGTON HOUSE, CHAPEL HILL, NC

Facing page: mellow brick buildings in Old Salem.
Above: Chocolate Mint Torte with Bourbon Crème Anglaise.

Flavor of
VIRGINIA

PARKE'S
SALAMAGUNDI

This attractive salad is an early summer favorite in Virginia.

PREPARATION TIME: 30 minutes
SERVES: 6-8

— I N G R E D I E N T S —

□ 1lb Virginia ham, julienned   □ 1lb chicken or turkey, julienned
□ 6 hard-boiled eggs, sliced   □ 8oz anchovy fillets   □ 4oz sardines in olive oil
□ Assorted pickles   □ Celery hearts   □ Assorted salad greens
□ 1 cup or more of your favorite French dressing

Arrange the meat and fish in a circular pattern on a large serving platter. Surround with the celery hearts, salad greens and pickles. Pour a light coating of French dressing over all just before serving.

WOODLAWN PLANTATION COOK BOOK,
JOAN SMITH, EDITOR,
MOUNT VERNON, VA

Previous pages: sunset over the Blue Ridge Mountains. Above: Parke's Salamagundi. Facing page: Seashore State Park is a 2,700-acre wilderness of forest, dune and swamp.

STUFFED SOFT-SHELL
CRAB IMPERIAL

This delicious dish uses some of the wonderful fresh seafood that makes Virginia famous.

PREPARATION TIME: 30 minutes

COOKING TIME: 10-12 minutes

SERVES: 6

INGREDIENTS

□ 6 soft-shell crabs

CRAB IMPERIAL MIXTURE

□ 1lb backfin crab meat   □ 1 egg   □ ⅓ cup mayonnaise
□ ¼ cup onion, finely diced   □ ⅓ tsp Worcestershire sauce
□ 1 tsp dry mustard   □ Pinch cayenne pepper

GARNISH

□ Parsley sprigs   □ Lemon wedges

To prepare the Crab Imperial mixture first remove the crab meat from the shell carefully to keep the meat in lump form. Set aside. In a separate bowl, beat the egg and combine with the mayonnaise. Set aside a quarter of this mixture to use as a topping. Add the remaining ingredients and toss with the crab meat.

Clean the soft-shell crabs by removing the gills and viscera. Fold back the top portion of the crabs and stuff with the Imperial mixture. Bake at 350°F for 10-12 minutes. Top with the reserved mayonnaise mixture and brown under the broiler. Garnish each with a sprig of parsley and a lemon wedge. Serve hot.

BRICE AND SHIRLEY PHILLIPS,
PHILLIPS WATERSIDE, NORFOLK, VA

Above: Stuffed Soft-Shell Crab Imperial. Facing page: these replicas of two historic ships are moored in Jamestown Festival Park. Overleaf: Smoked Tuna Salad.

SMOKED TUNA SALAD

This makes an elegant and delicious luncheon salad. If you don't have champagne vinegar, try using a herb vinegar instead.

PREPARATION TIME: 15 minutes

MARINATING TIME: 1-2 hours

SERVES: 4-6

INGREDIENTS

- ☐ 8oz smoked tuna   ☐ 8oz can artichoke hearts, drained and quartered
- ☐ ½ red pepper, thinly sliced   ☐ 4 leaves fresh basil, finely chopped
- ☐ 3 scallions, sliced   ☐ 1 tomato, diced
- ☐ ¼ cup Extra Virgin olive oil, or more to taste
- ☐ ⅛ cup champagne vinegar, or more to taste

TO SERVE

- ☐ Fresh salad greens

Combine the artichoke hearts, pepper, basil, scallions and tomato. Toss lightly with the olive oil. Season with salt and pepper and gently toss again with the champagne vinegar. Allow the mixture to marinate for 1-2 hours before adding the smoked tuna. Toss lightly to combine and serve on a bed of fresh salad greens.

SUSAN PAINTER,
THE SHIP'S CABIN SEAFOOD RESTAURANT,
NORFOLK, VA

GRILLED SEAFOOD
BROCHETTES

Use the freshest seafood you can find to make these colorful brochettes. They make wonderful fare at a summer barbecue. Serve with boiled rice and a sauce of hot lemon caper butter.

PREPARATION TIME: 30 minutes

COOKING TIME: 10 minutes

SERVES: 6

─────────────── I N G R E D I E N T S ───────────────

☐ 3 lemons, cut into quarters ☐ 9oz salmon, cut into 6 pieces
☐ 3 small tomatoes, cut into quarters ☐ 12 large shrimp
☐ 3 small green peppers, cut into quarters ☐ 9oz swordfish, cut into 6 pieces
☐ 6 large mushrooms ☐ 12 large scallops
☐ 3 6oz lobster tails, cut in half ☐ Vegetable oil

Coat 6 skewers with a small amount of vegetable oil to prevent sticking and divide the seafood and vegetables among the skewers. Make sure that you place the skewers through the center of the pieces. Grill over a hot charcoal for 5-10 minutes, or until the ingredients are tender.

JOE HOGGARD,
THE SHIP'S CABIN SEAFOOD RESTAURANT,
NORFOLK, VA

Above: Grilled Seafood Brochettes. Facing page: azaleas provide a colorful backdrop to a Japanese-style garden of raked gravel.

LORENZO'S COUNTRY HAM

PREPARATION TIME: 15 minutes
SOAKING TIME: 12 hours or more
COOKING TIME: 12 hours or overnight
SERVES: 3 per lb

INGREDIENTS

☐ 1 whole country ham, uncooked   ☐ 4 cups water   ☐ ½ cup sugar
☐ 1 cup fine dry bread crumbs

TO COOK

☐ Heavy duty aluminum foil

Soak the ham for 12 hours or longer. Wash thoroughly and scrub off all of the mold. Preheat the oven to 400°F. Place the ham on a large sheet of heavy duty aluminum foil and put in a roasting pan. Join the sides of the foil to form a container. Pour in the water and seal the top of the foil. Roast for 20 minutes, then turn off the oven for 3 hours, leaving the ham inside and the oven door closed. Reheat the oven to 400°F and, when it has come up to temperature, roast for a further 20 minutes. Turn off the oven again and leave the ham inside for 6-8 hours or overnight. Do not open the oven door during the entire cooking cycle. When the cooking time is up, remove the ham from the foil and, while still warm, carefully remove the skin and all but a very thin layer of the fat. Sprinkle the ham with the sugar and bread crumbs and bake, uncovered, at 400°F for 15 minutes, or until the ham is nicely browned. Cool and slice as thinly as possible to serve.

   Leftover ham can be stored in the refrigerator, wrapped in foil or plastic for 3 weeks or more. Eternity has been defined as two people and a ham, but you will find any leftover ham so delicious in casseroles and soups that you will wish it could last for ever!

WOODLAWN PLANTATION COOK BOOK,
JOAN SMITH, EDITOR,
MOUNT VERNON, VA

*Above: Lorenzo's Country Ham. Facing page: the apothecary's building at
James Fort, the first permanent English settlement in America.*

GREY'S HILL ROAST TURKEY WITH CORNBREAD STUFFING

A stuffed holiday bird with a definite Southern accent.

PREPARATION TIME: 30 minutes

COOKING TIME: 4½-5 hours

SERVES: 12-15

INGREDIENTS

CORNBREAD STUFFING

☐ 2 tbsps butter   ☐ ½ cup chopped onion   ☐ 2 tbsps chopped celery
☐ 2 tbsps green pepper   ☐ 2 cups corn bread cubes   ☐ 1 cup bread cubes
☐ 1 tbsp chopped parsley   ☐ Salt to taste   ☐ Pinch thyme
☐ ½ cup or more chicken stock or water

ROAST TURKEY

☐ 10-12lb turkey at room temperature
☐ 2 tsps baking soda   ☐ 2 tsps salt   ☐ 1 tsp pepper   ☐ 2 tbsps butter, softened
☐ 4 tbsps butter, melted   ☐ ½ cup cognac

First prepare the stuffing. Melt the butter and sauté the onion, pepper and celery until tender. Stir in the remaining stuffing ingredients and moisten with chicken stock or hot water.

Preheat the oven to 450°F. Wash and dry the turkey. Rub the inside of the body and neck with salt, baking soda and pepper. Lightly stuff the cavities with the cornbread stuffing and sew or skewer closed. Tuck the wings under and fasten the legs down. Rub the surface of the bird with the softened butter and place on a rack in a shallow baking pan, breast side up. Combine the melted butter and cognac to use as a baste. Place the turkey in the preheated oven and immediately reduce the heat to 325°F. Roast uncovered for 1 hour, basting frequently. Make a loose tent out of aluminum foil and lay on top of the bird. Continue cooking for a further 3 hours, basting from time to time. If you run out of the baste, pour some boiling water into the bottom of the roasting pan, stir up the drippings and use this liquid as a baste. Remove the foil during the last 30 minutes to allow the bird to brown. The turkey is done when the leg joint moves freely. Remove from the oven and allow the bird to stand for 20 minutes before carving.

RIDGEWELL CATERER, INC.
WOODLAWN PLANTATION COOK BOOK,
JOAN SMITH, EDITOR,
MOUNT VERNON, VA

Facing Page: Grey's Hill Roast Turkey with Cornbread Stuffing.

JOAN SMITH'S THANKSGIVING PIE

Try this marvellous version of pumpkin pie for your next holiday feast.

PREPARATION TIME: 1 hour
COOKING TIME: 1 hour and 15 minutes
SERVES: 6-8

INGREDIENTS

NUT MERINGUE SHELL

☐ ½ cup walnuts or pecans, ground ☐ 3 egg whites ☐ ¼ tsp cream of tartar
☐ ⅛ tsp salt ☐ 1 cup sugar ☐ ½ tsp cinnamon

PUMPKIN CHIFFON FILLING

☐ 1 cup walnuts or pecans, ground ☐ 1 tbsp plain gelatine
☐ ¼ cup sherry or dark rum ☐ ⅔ cup brown sugar, packed
☐ ½ tsp salt ☐ 1 tsp cinnamon ☐ ½ tsp nutmeg ☐ ½ tsp ginger
☐ 3 eggs, separated ☐ ¾ cup milk ☐ 1 cup cooked puréed pumpkin
☐ ⅓ cup sugar

TOPPING

☐ 1 cup heavy cream ☐ 1 tbsp sugar ☐ ¼ cup dark rum

Above: Monticello, dating from 1769, was the home of Thomas Jefferson.

To prepare the meringue shell, first preheat the oven to 275°F. Beat the egg whites with the cream of tartar and salt until they form soft peaks. Gradually add the sugar, about 2 tablespoons at a time, until the meringue stands up in stiff, glossy peaks. Beat in the cinnamon along with the last ¼ cup of sugar. Gently fold in the nuts. Pile the meringue onto a lightly-greased 9-inch pie plate. Spread it over the bottom to approximately ¼-inch thickness and up the sides to form a crust. Bake for 50-60 minutes until the shell is a light tan color. Turn off the oven and leave the meringue to cool with the door closed. The meringue will crack and fall in the center. When the meringue is cool, press the center lightly to make a shell.

To prepare the filling, soften the gelatine in the sherry or rum. Combine with the brown sugar, salt, spices, beaten egg yolks and milk. Cook and stir over a low heat until the mixture thickens, about 10 minutes. Remove from the heat and stir in the pumpkin. Chill until the mixture is very thick. Meanwhile, beat the egg whites to soft peaks and gradually beat in the sugar to form a meringue. Fold the meringue into the pumpkin mixture along with ⅔ cup of the nuts. Spoon the filling into the cooled meringue shell and sprinkle the remaining nuts around the edge. Chill until firm.

To prepare the topping, beat the cream to soft peaks, add the sugar and stir in the rum. Add a large spoonfull to each serving of pie.

RIDGEWELL CATERER, INC.
WOODLAWN PLANTATION COOK BOOK,
JOAN SMITH, EDITOR,
MOUNT VERNON, VA

Above: Joan Smith's Thanksgiving Pie.

NELLY CUSTIS'
MAIDS OF HONOR

These popular treats originally came from England, but were very popular in early America.

PREPARATION TIME: 20 minutes

COOKING TIME: 45 minutes

YIELD: 8-10 tarts

─────────────── I N G R E D I E N T S ───────────────

☐ Pastry to line 8-10 3½-inch tart pans ☐ 2 eggs ☐ ½ cup sugar
☐ ½ cup almond paste ☐ 1-2 tbsps sherry ☐ 2 tbsps melted butter
☐ 1 tbsp lemon juice ☐ 2 tbsps flour ☐ 8-10 tsps strawberry or raspberry jam

Preheat the oven to 350°F. Use the pastry to line the tart pans and arrange them on a baking sheet. Beat the eggs until very light and fluffy. Gradually beat in the sugar. Soften the almond paste with the sherry, butter and lemon juice. Add this mixture to the beaten eggs. Drop 1 teaspoon of jam into each tart shell and fill with the batter. Bake for about 45 minutes, or until puffed, golden and firm.

RIDGEWELL CATERER, INC.
WOODLAWN PLANTATION COOK BOOK,
JOAN SMITH, EDITOR,
MOUNT VERNON, VA

Above: an unusual view of the Blue Ridge Mountains. Facing page: Nelly Custis' Maids of Honor.

APPLE TORTE

*Serve this delicious dessert warm or cold with vanilla
ice cream.*

PREPARATION TIME: 20 minutes
COOKING TIME: 45 minutes
SERVES: 6-8

──── I N G R E D I E N T S ────

- ⅔ cup flour, sifted   □ 3 tsps baking powder   □ ½ tsp salt
- □ 2 eggs, beaten   □ 1½ cups sugar   □ 3 tsps vanilla
- □ 2 cups apples, peeled, cored and diced
- □ 1 cup pecans or walnuts, chopped

Preheat the oven to 350°F. Sift together the flour, baking powder and salt. Set aside. In a separate bowl, combine the sugar, vanilla and beaten eggs. Stir in the dry ingredients, apples and nuts. Pour the batter into a buttered 8x12x4-inch baking dish. Bake for 45 minutes or until a knife inserted in the center comes out clean.

RIDGEWELL CATERER, INC.
WOODLAWN PLANTATION COOK BOOK,
JOAN SMITH, EDITOR,
MOUNT VERNON, VA

*Facing page: a blaze of spring color in the Norfolk Botanical Gardens.
Above: Apple Torte.*

Flavor of
KENTUCKY

TOMATO CELERY SOUP

The addition of the fresh vegetables makes canned tomato soup taste homemade.

PREPARATION TIME: 15 minutes

COOKING TIME: 5 minutes

SERVES: 4

INGREDIENTS

- ☐ 1 small onion, chopped
- ☐ ½ cup finely chopped celery
- ☐ 2 tbsps butter
- ☐ 1 10½ oz can of tomato soup
- ☐ 1 can water
- ☐ 1 tsp chopped parsley
- ☐ 1 tbsp lemon juice
- ☐ 1 tsp sugar
- ☐ ¼ tsp salt
- ☐ ⅛ tsp pepper

GARNISH

- ☐ ¼ cup unsweetened cream, whipped
- ☐ Chopped parsley

Sauté the onion and celery in the butter, but do not brown. Add the tomato soup, water, parsley, lemon juice, sugar, salt and pepper. Simmer for 5 minutes. The celery will remain crisp. To serve, pour into 4 bowls and top each with a spoonful of unsweetened whipped cream and a sprinkling of chopped parsley.

COURTESY ELIZABETH C. KREMER
FROM THE TRUSTEES HOUSE DAILY
FARE, PLEASANT HILL, KENTUCKY
PLEASANT HILL PRESS, HARRODSBURG,
KENTUCKY 1970 AND 1977

Previous pages: Kentucky's famous bluegrass country. Above: Tomato Celery Soup. Facing page: a Kentucky cornfield near Barbourville.

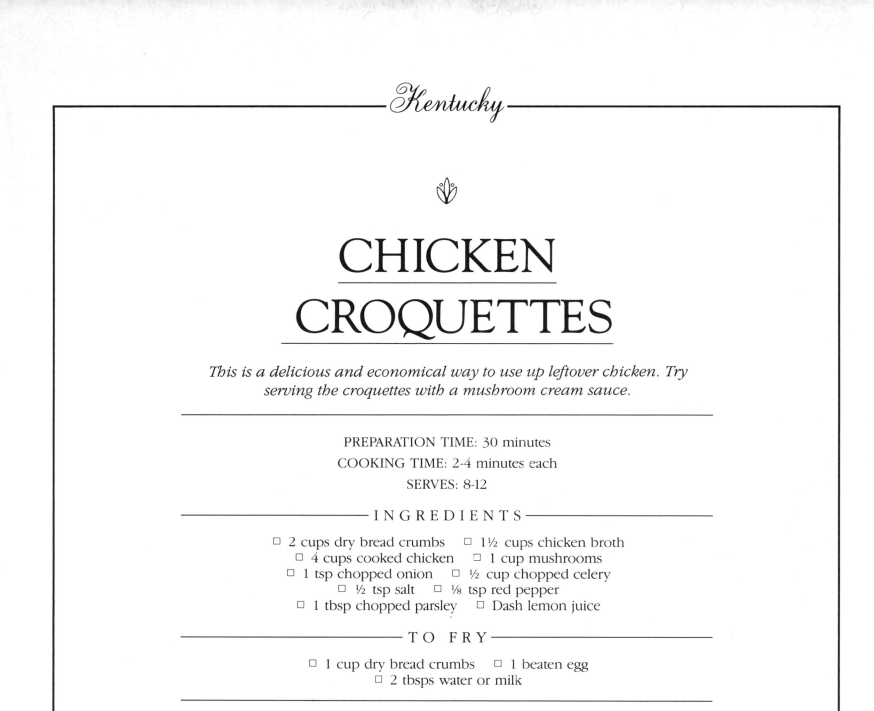

CHICKEN
CROQUETTES

This is a delicious and economical way to use up leftover chicken. Try serving the croquettes with a mushroom cream sauce.

PREPARATION TIME: 30 minutes

COOKING TIME: 2-4 minutes each

SERVES: 8-12

INGREDIENTS

- ☐ 2 cups dry bread crumbs
- ☐ 1½ cups chicken broth
- ☐ 4 cups cooked chicken
- ☐ 1 cup mushrooms
- ☐ 1 tsp chopped onion
- ☐ ½ cup chopped celery
- ☐ ½ tsp salt
- ☐ ⅛ tsp red pepper
- ☐ 1 tbsp chopped parsley
- ☐ Dash lemon juice

TO FRY

- ☐ 1 cup dry bread crumbs
- ☐ 1 beaten egg
- ☐ 2 tbsps water or milk

Soak the bread crumbs in the broth. Meanwhile, grind together the chicken and mushrooms, Combine with the soaked bread crumbs and the rest of the ingredients and allow to cool. Shape into 24 croquettes and chill. To cook, dip each croquette into dry bread crumbs, then into a mixture of beaten egg and water or milk, and finally into bread crumbs again. (This is the secret of good croquettes!) Fry in deep fat, heated to around 375°F, or until a 1 inch cube of bread browns in 1 minute, until golden (approximately 2-4 minutes).

COURTESY ELIZABETH C. KREMER
FROM THE TRUSTEES HOUSE DAILY
FARE, PLEASANT HILL, KENTUCKY
PLEASANT HILL PRESS, HARRODSBURG,
KENTUCKY 1970 AND 1977

Facing page: Chicken Croquettes give a new twist to Kentucky fried chicken.

KENTUCKY COUNTRY
HAM

Country ham is sugar cured, smoked and hung for up to 18 months to develop its full flavor. Don't worry about the exterior mold. It is harmless and is scrubbed off before cooking.

PREPARATION TIME: 30 minutes
COOKING TIME: 1 hour 20 minutes, plus 20 minutes per lb
SERVES: 3-4 people per lb

INGREDIENTS

- □ 1 country ham □ ½ cup whole cloves
- □ 1 cup brown sugar □ 1 cup vinegar
- □ 1½ gallons water

GLAZE

- □ 1 cup brown sugar □ 1 cup cornmeal
- □ 1 tbsp ground cloves □ 1 tsp cinnamon

Scrub the ham well to remove the exterior mold and soak overnight in the water. Sprinkle half of the cloves into the bottom of a roasting tin, place the ham on top, and sprinkle the remaining cloves on top of the ham. Bake for 1 hour at 375°F, then reduce the temperature to 275°F and cook for 20 minutes per pound, or until an internal temperature of 150°F is reached. When the ham is fully cooked, remove from the roasting tin, trim if necessary and bone if desired. Wash the roasting tin and replace the cooked ham. Prepare the glaze by combining the brown sugar, cornmeal and spices. Sprinkle this mixture over the ham and brown in the oven at 375°F until the glaze has melted.

COURTESY ELIZABETH C. KREMER
FROM THE TRUSTEES HOUSE DAILY
FARE, PLEASANT HILL, KENTUCKY
PLEASANT HILL PRESS, HARRODSBURG,
KENTUCKY 1970 AND 1977

Facing page: this grazing thoroughbred is a reminder of Kentucky's reputation for quality horsebreeding. Above: Kentucky Country Ham.

SCALLOPED OYSTER PLANT

The oyster plant, also known as salsify, is a root vegetable with a delicate oyster-like flavor.

PREPARATION TIME: 30 minutes
COOKING TIME: 30 minutes
SERVES: 4-6

INGREDIENTS

- 1 large oyster plant
- 2 cups bread or cracker crumbs
- 2 tbsps butter
- 1 cup cream

TOPPING

- 1 cup bread crumbs
- 4 tbsps butter

Slice the oyster plant into water to which you have added a little vinegar in order to prevent discoloration. Drain, then cook in fresh boiling water until tender and drain well. Arrange alternate layers of cooked oyster plant and cracker crumbs in a greased baking dish, beginning with a cracker crumb layer and ending with a layer of oyster plant. Dot each layer with butter and seasonings. Pour over the cream.

To prepare the topping, melt the butter in a saucepan and stir in the bread crumbs. Spread this mixture on top of the layers and bake at 400°F for approximately 30 minutes, or until the liquid is absorbed.

COURTESY ELIZABETH C. KREMER
FROM THE TRUSTEES HOUSE DAILY
FARE, PLEASANT HILL, KENTUCKY
PLEASANT HILL PRESS, HARRODSBURG,
KENTUCKY 1970 AND 1977

Above: looking over the Cumberland Falls.
Facing page: this old gristmill lies deep within a wood in Jefferson County.

CORN STICKS

All the secrets of good corn bread are revealed in this recipe!

PREPARATION TIME: 10 minutes
COOKING TIME: 10 minutes
YIELD: approximately 12 sticks

INGREDIENTS

☐ 1 cup + 2 tbsps cornmeal   ☐ ½ cup flour
☐ 3 tsps sugar   ☐ ½ tsp baking soda
☐ ½ tsp baking powder   ☐ ½ tsp salt
☐ 2 tbsps oil   ☐ 1 cup buttermilk
☐ 1 egg

Mix together the dry ingredients, then beat in the oil, egg and buttermilk. One of the secrets of good corn bread is to beat very well. Heat greased irons until hot enough to sizzle (this is the other secret of making good corn bread) and fill to half full. Bake at 450°F for about 10 minutes, or until brown.

COURTESY ELIZABETH C. KREMER FROM
THE TRUSTEES HOUSE DAILY
FARE, PLEASANT HILL, KENTUCKY,
PLEASANT HILL PRESS, HARRODSBURG,
KENTUCKY 1970 AND 1977

Facing page: these Kentucky fields provide the chief ingredient for Corn Sticks.

PLEASANT HILL BAKED EGGPLANT

The creamy filling makes an attractive contrast against the brilliant purple of the eggplants. You could substitute summer squash for the eggplant if you wish.

PREPARATION TIME: 30 minutes
COOKING TIME: 30-35 minutes
SERVES: 4-6

INGREDIENTS

☐ 1 large eggplant

FILLING

☐ ½ medium onion, chopped ☐ 3 tbsps butter
☐ 3 tbsps chopped parsley ☐ 1 10½ oz can cream of mushroom soup
☐ 1-2 cups unsalted butter crackers, crushed ☐ Dash of Worcestershire sauce
☐ Salt and pepper to taste

Cut off the top of the eggplant and scrape out the inside, leaving about ½ inch around the sides and bottom of the shell. Boil the eggplant flesh in salted water until tender. Drain well and chop. Sauté the chopped onion in 2 tablespoons butter and add the parsley. Mix in the cooked eggplant, soup and seasonings. Add enough cracker crumbs to make a good stuffing consistency. Pile the mixture into the eggplant shell, sprinkle with cracker crumbs and dot with the remaining tablespoon of butter. Bake at 375°F for 30-35 minutes, or until the eggplant is soft.

COURTESY ELIZABETH C. KREMER
FROM THE TRUSTEES HOUSE DAILY FARE,
PLEASANT HILL, KENTUCKY
PLEASANT HILL PRESS, HARRODSBURG,
KENTUCKY 1970 AND 1977

Facing page: Rock Bridge Arch, which spans Red River Gorge in Wolfe County, is the result of erosion over millions of years.

SHAKER LEMON PIE

This tart and refreshing pie is unusual in that it uses the whole lemon, not just the juice.

PREPARATION TIME: 30 minutes plus standing time
COOKING TIME: 35 minutes
SERVES: 6-8

INGREDIENTS

PASTRY

☐ 2 cups all-purpose flour   ☐ 1 tsp salt
☐ ⅓ cup shortening   ☐ ⅓ cup butter, chilled
☐ 5 tbsps cold water

FILLING

☐ 2 large lemons   ☐ 4 eggs, well beaten
☐ 2 cups sugar

To prepare the pastry, combine the butter and salt in a bowl. Cut in the shortening and butter until the mixture resembles coarse bread crumbs. Gradually sprinkle on the cold water and blend lightly with a fork, until you can just gather the dough into a ball. Divide the dough into 2 pieces and leave to rest in a cool place for at least ½ hour. Roll out one of the pieces and line a 9-inch pie plate. Roll out the second piece to form a top crust.

To make the filling, wash the lemons and slice them paper thin, rind and all. Cover with the sugar and let stand for at least two hours, overnight is better, stirring occasionally. Add the beaten eggs and mix well. Turn the filling into the lined pie dish. Cover with the top crust and cut several slits near the center. Bake at 450°F for 15 minutes, then reduce heat to 375°F and bake for about 20 minutes or until a knife inserted near the edge of the pie comes out clean. Cool before serving.

COURTESY ELIZABETH C. KREMER
FROM THE TRUSTEES HOUSE DAILY FARE,
PLEASANT HILL, KENTUCKY PLEASANT
HILL PRESS, HARRODSBURG, KENTUCKY
1970 AND 1977

Above: Shaker Lemon Pie. Facing page: the wide skies of central Kentucky show off a spectacular sunset to the full.

Flavor of
TENNESSEE

SQUASH SIDE DISH

PREPARATION TIME: 20 minutes

COOKING TIME: 15 minutes

SERVES: 8

INGREDIENTS

☐ 3 tbsps butter   ☐ 1 medium onion, chopped   ☐ 1 medium bell pepper, diced
☐ 2 medium zucchini squash, sliced
☐ 2 medium yellow summer squash, sliced   ☐ 14½ oz can tomato wedges
☐ ½ tsp garlic salt   ☐ Salt and pepper to taste

GARNISH

☐ Fresh parsley   ☐ Grated Parmesan cheese

Melt the butter in a heavy skillet, add the onion and cook until transparent. Stir in the bell pepper and continue cooking until soft. Add the squash and seasonings, cover, and simmer until just tender. Drain the tomatoes, reserving the liquid, and add them to the skillet. Cook for an additional 5 to 8 minutes, adding some of the reserved liquid if needed.

Garnish this colorful dish with parsley and sprinkle with Parmesan cheese before serving.

DORIS BELCHER, MEMPHIS, TN

*Previous pages: the Old Mill, Pigeon Forge. Above: Squash Side Dish. Facing
page: a view of Cheekwood in Nashville.*

TRIPLE BEAN SALAD
PIQUANT

This super salad is so easy to make, and sure to please!

PREPARATION TIME: 10 minutes

COOKING TIME: 8 hours or overnight

SERVES: 8-10

──────── INGREDIENTS ────────

☐ 1 16oz can wax beans, drained ☐ 1 16oz can cut green beans, drained
☐ 1 16oz can dark red large kidney beans, drained
☐ ½ cup sliced celery ☐ 1 medium bell pepper, deseeded and diced
☐ 1 medium sweet onion, sliced into rings ☐ ½ cup sugar
☐ ½ cup salad oil ☐ ¾ cup cider or wine vinegar

Toss the vegetables together in a large salad bowl. Combine the sugar, oil and vinegar and pour over the vegetables. Allow to marinate, refrigerated, for 8 hours or overnight. Toss the vegetables to distribute the dressing before serving.

DORIS BELCHER, MEMPHIS, TN

*Facing page: seen from Mud Island, the setting sun turns the Mississippi River
to liquid gold. Above: Triple Bean Salad Piquant.*

CURRY DIP

Serve this tasty dip with a selection of raw vegetables such as carrot and celery sticks, sliced squash, and broccoli flowerets.

PREPARATION TIME: 10 minutes

COOKING TIME: overnight

YIELD: approximately 2 cups

————————— I N G R E D I E N T S —————————

☐ 1 cup mayonnaise   ☐ 3oz cream cheese, softened   ☐ 1 tsp tarragon vinegar
☐ ½ tsp prepared horseradish   ☐ ½ tsp garlic salt
☐ 1 tsp curry powder

Combine all the ingredients and chill the dip in the refrigerator overnight. If the dip is too stiff, add a small amount of milk to soften.

DORIS BELCHER, MEMPHIS, TN

PICKLED OKRA

With this tasty pickle in your store cupboard you will always have a crunchy snack ready to serve to unexpected guests.

PREPARATION TIME: 30 minutes

COOKING TIME: 10 minutes

YIELD: approximately 6 pints

————————— I N G R E D I E N T S —————————

☐ 3 cups white vinegar   ☐ 3 cups water   ☐ 1½ cups sugar
☐ 6 cloves garlic   ☐ 5lbs small to medium okra, trimmed
☐ Salt (non-iodized)

To prepare the okra for pickling, remove the stem and trim the top of the pod. Pack the okra and garlic into sterilized pint jars. Combine the vinegar, water and sugar in a saucepan and bring to the boil. Pour over the okra and add ½ tsp salt to each pint. Seal the jars and process for 10 minutes in a boiling water bath.

DORIS BELCHER, MEMPHIS, TN

Facing page: Curry Dip is ideal for easy, summer eating.

ALL AMERICAN
POTATO SALAD

Here is a delicious salad to serve with the Triple Bean Salad Piquant
for a gorgeous summer meal.

PREPARATION TIME: 15 minutes

COOKING TIME: 2 hours or more

SERVES: 8

INGREDIENTS

□ 4 cups diced cold boiled potatoes   □ 1-2 tbsps minced onion
□ ¼ cup celery, chopped (optional)   □ 2 tbsps chopped pimento
□ ½ cup mayonnaise   □ ¼ cup chopped dill pickle   □ ½ tsp prepared mustard
□ ½ tsp salt   □ Pepper to taste
□ 2-3 hard-boiled eggs, coarsely chopped

Combine all the ingredients except for the eggs, and toss carefully until well mixed. Add the eggs, reserving some for a garnish, and mix gently. Garnish the salad with the reserved eggs and chill for at least 2 hours before serving.

DORIS BELCHER, MEMPHIS, TN

Above: All American Potato Salad. Facing page: seen at twilight, the Great
Smoky Mountains appear blue in the distance.

BARBECUE CHICKEN

Here is a delicious alternative to Southern Fried Chicken.

PREPARATION TIME: 20 minutes

COOKING TIME: 1 hour 20 minutes

SERVES: 4

INGREDIENTS

☐ 1 fryer chicken (about 2½ lbs), cut into pieces
☐ ½ cup flour   ☐ Salt and pepper

SAUCE

☐ 1 medium onion, chopped   ☐ 2 tbsps vegetable oil
☐ 2 tbsps vinegar   ☐ 2 tbsps brown sugar   ☐ ¼ cup lemon juice
☐ 1 cup ketchup   ☐ 3 tbsps Worcestershire sauce
☐ ½ tbsp prepared mustard   ☐ 1 cup water   ☐ Dash Tabasco sauce

Shake the chicken pieces in a paper bag containing the flour, salt and pepper. Brown in a heavy skillet using a small amount of vegetable oil. Drain off any excess oil and place the chicken in a shallow baking pan. Set aside while you prepare the sauce. To make the sauce, brown the onion in the vegetable oil in a heavy skillet. Add the remaining sauce ingredients and simmer for 20 minutes. Pour the sauce over the chicken and bake, uncovered, at 325°F for 1 hour, or until the chicken is tender. Baste frequently with the sauce during the cooking time.

DORIS BELCHER, MEMPHIS, TN

Facing page: built in 1770, this house forms part of the settlement at Rocky Mount. Above: Barbecue Chicken.

TENNESSEE RIBS

The long cooking over hickory charcoal and the frequent basting with the sweet sauce make these ribs something special.

PREPARATION TIME: 20 minutes

COOKING TIME: approximately 2 hours

SERVES: 6

INGREDIENTS

☐ 4-5lbs spare ribs

SAUCE

☐ 8oz can tomato sauce   ☐ ½ cup sherry   ☐ ½ cup honey
☐ 2 tbsps wine vinegar   ☐ 2 tbsps onion, minced
☐ 1 clove garlic, minced   ☐ ¼ tsp Worcestershire sauce

Arrange the ribs in a shallow roasting pan and bake at 350°F for 30 minutes. Meanwhile, in a saucepan, combine the sauce ingredients and simmer for 5 minutes. Prepare a fire in a barbecue using hickory charcoal. Push the coals to one side of the grill and, when the coals are ashed over, place the ribs on the part of the grill which is away from the coals. Grill indirectly in this way for about 45 minutes, then move the ribs directly over the coals. Brush them frequently with the sauce as you continue to grill them for a further 20-30 minutes.

MARY ANN FOWLKES, NASHVILLE, TN

MARINATED
CUCUMBERS

PREPARATION TIME: 20 minutes
SERVES: 8

── INGREDIENTS ──

□ 4 cucumbers, sliced   □ 1 small onion, thinly sliced
□ ¼ cup sugar   □ ⅔ cup vinegar
□ ½ tsp celery seed   □ 1½ tsps salt

Combine the cucumber and onion slices. Sprinkle with the salt and sugar, then add the vinegar and celery seed. Mix thoroughly to combine. Cover and chill until ready to serve. Garnish this crisp, cool salad with slivers of red radishes for a lovely summery contrast.

PAT COKER, NASHVILLE, TN

Facing page: at 256 feet Fall Creek Falls is the highest waterfall in the Eastern United States. Above: Tennessee Ribs form the centerpiece of this outdoor feast.

TENNESSEE
FRIED CORN

Use really fresh corn to obtain the full flavor of this delicious dish.

PREPARATION TIME: 30 minutes

COOKING TIME: 20 minutes

SERVES: 4

INGREDIENTS

☐ 2 cups fresh corn (6-8 ears) ☐ 5 tbsps butter and bacon drippings, mixed
☐ 1 tsp sugar ☐ 1-1½ cups water ☐ Salt and pepper to taste

Select corn which has full, round, milky kernels. Remove the shucks and the silk. Run a sharp knife along the ears to cut off the tips of the kernels, then scrape the edge of the knife along the cob to remove all of the milky portion which remains. Heat the fat in a heavy skillet. Add the corn, water, sugar, salt and pepper. Stir constantly to heat through. Lower the heat and cook, stirring frequently, until the corn is thickened and almost transparent in color. This will take about 15-20 minutes.

CALLIE LILLIE OWEN,
COURTESY NASHVILLE COOKBOOK

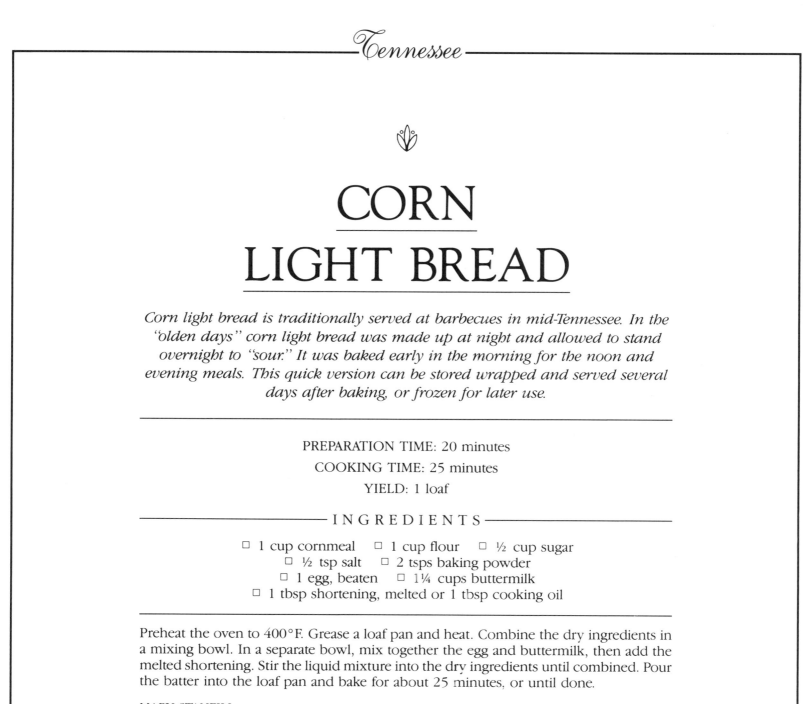

CORN
LIGHT BREAD

Corn light bread is traditionally served at barbecues in mid-Tennessee. In the "olden days" corn light bread was made up at night and allowed to stand overnight to "sour." It was baked early in the morning for the noon and evening meals. This quick version can be stored wrapped and served several days after baking, or frozen for later use.

PREPARATION TIME: 20 minutes

COOKING TIME: 25 minutes

YIELD: 1 loaf

INGREDIENTS

☐ 1 cup cornmeal   ☐ 1 cup flour   ☐ ½ cup sugar
☐ ½ tsp salt   ☐ 2 tsps baking powder
☐ 1 egg, beaten   ☐ 1¼ cups buttermilk
☐ 1 tbsp shortening, melted or 1 tbsp cooking oil

Preheat the oven to 400°F. Grease a loaf pan and heat. Combine the dry ingredients in a mixing bowl. In a separate bowl, mix together the egg and buttermilk, then add the melted shortening. Stir the liquid mixture into the dry ingredients until combined. Pour the batter into the loaf pan and bake for about 25 minutes, or until done.

MARY STANFILL,
COURTESY OF NASHVILLE COOKBOOK

*Facing page: dead tree trunks add to the eerie atmosphere of this landscape.
Above: Rocky Mount settlement.*

ANGEL BISCUITS

Angel biscuits are like their name – heavenly!

PREPARATION TIME: 20 minutes
COOKING TIME: 10-12 minutes
YIELD: approximately 50 biscuits

INGREDIENTS

- ☐ 5 cups all-purpose flour
- ☐ 1 tsp baking powder
- ☐ 1 tsp salt
- ☐ ¾ cup vegetable shortening
- ☐ 2 cups milk
- ☐ 2 tbsps sugar
- ☐ 1 package yeast (about 1oz)
- ☐ ½ cup warm water

Sift together the flour, baking powder and salt and cut in the shortening with two knives or a pastry cutter until the mixture resembles coarse bread crumbs. Dissolve the yeast in the warm water and stir in the sugar. Add the yeast along with the milk to the dry ingredients and stir until the mixture is moist. To make biscuits, roll the dough onto a floured surface to a ½-inch thickness. Cut with a biscuit cutter and bake on greased baking sheets. Bake at 400°F for 10-12 minutes, or until the biscuits are lightly browned. If you prefer, the dough may be stored, covered, in the refrigerator for up to one week and baked as needed.

DORIS BELCHER, MEMPHIS, TN

Above: water is no longer a small scale source of power and the old mill wheels are idle. Facing page: Angel Biscuits and Good Morning Coffee Cake.

GOOD MORNING

COFFEE CAKE

If you know this coffee cake is waiting, getting up should
be no problem.

PREPARATION TIME: 20 minutes

COOKING TIME: 25-30 minutes

YIELD: 8-inch-square cake

INGREDIENTS

☐ 1½ cups self-rising flour or
1½ cups all-purpose flour, ½ tsp salt and 2 tsps baking powder
☐ ½ cup sugar   ☐ 1 egg, beaten   ☐ ½ cup milk
☐ 3 tbsps vegetable oil

STREUSEL TOPPING

☐ ¼ cup flour   ☐ ¼ cup sugar   ☐ ½ tsp cinnamon
☐ 2 tbsps butter   ☐ 2 red apples, unpeeled and cut into eighths

To make the cake, sift together the flour and sugar. In a separate bowl, mix the egg, milk and oil. Gradually add this liquid to the dry ingredients, stirring until the batter is smooth. Pour the mixture into a greased 8-inch square or a 9-inch round pan. Set aside while you prepare the Streusel Topping. To make the topping, combine the flour, sugar and cinnamon in a bowl. Cut in the butter until the mixture resembles coarse crumbs. Sprinkle over the batter and arrange the apple slices in a circle on top. Bake at 400°F for 25-30 minutes or until a knife inserted in the center comes out clean. Serve hot.

DORIS BELCHER, MEMPHIS, TN

FRESH FRUIT
COBBLER

Serve this tempting dessert warm with cream or whipped cream. You can vary the fruit to suit the season.

PREPARATION TIME: 30 minutes

COOKING TIME: 30 minutes

SERVES: 6-8

INGREDIENTS

☐ ¾-1 cup sugar   ☐ 1 tbsp cornstarch   ☐ 1 cup water
☐ 3½ cups sliced fresh fruit (for example apples, peaches or berries, plus juice)
☐ ½ tbsp butter   ☐ Pinch cinnamon

PASTRY

☐ 1 cup all-purpose flour   ☐ ⅓ tsp salt
☐ ⅓ cup plus 1 tbsp shortening   ☐ 2-3 tbsps cold water
☐ ½ tbsp butter, melted   ☐ Pinch cinnamon

Combine the sugar, cornstarch and water and bring to a boil. Boil for 1 minute, then add the fruit and juice and cook for a further minute. Pour into a well buttered 1½-quart baking dish. Sprinkle lightly with the cinnamon and dot with the butter. Prepare the pastry by combining the flour and salt. Cut in the shortening until the mixture resembles coarse crumbs. Sprinkle in the water and mix gently until the dough can be formed into a soft ball. Roll out on a floured surface to a ⅛-inch thickness. Cut the dough into ½-inch-wide strips and arrange in a lattice pattern over the fruit. Brush the pastry with melted butter, sprinkle with cinnamon and bake at 400°F for 30 minutes, or until the cobbler is golden brown and bubbly.

DORIS BELCHER, MEMPHIS, TN

Facing page: early evening at Pickwick Landing. Above: Fresh Fruit Cobbler.

Flavor of
ALABAMA

SOUTHERN-STYLE

POTATO SOUP

Makes a refreshing soup on a hot day.

PREPARATION TIME: 30 minutes, plus chilling
COOKING TIME: approximately 50 minutes
YIELD: 1½ quarts

INGREDIENTS

- 1½ cups green onions, white part only, diced
- ½ cup onions, chopped □ 1 tbsp butter
- 3 cups baking potatoes, peeled and diced
- 3 cups hot water □ 3 tsps salt
- 1 cup hot milk □ ½ tsp white pepper
- 1 cup light cream □ 1 cup heavy cream
- 8 tsps chopped chives

In a heavy 4-quart pot, sauté the onions in the butter until soft, but not brown. Add the potatoes, hot water and 2 tsps of the salt. Simmer, uncovered, for 30-40 minutes, or until the potatoes are soft. Liquidize the potatoes and onions, and return to the pot. Add the hot milk, and slowly bring the soup to a boil, stirring often to keep the potatoes from settling. Add the remaining salt and the pepper. Remove from the heat and strain through a sieve. Cool the soup, stir, then strain again and add the light and heavy cream. Serve chilled and garnished with the chopped chives.

STURDIVANT MUSEUM ASSOCIATION,
SELMA, AL

Previous pages: DeSoto Falls State Park. Facing page: Southern-Style Potato Soup.

BUTTER BEAN SALAD

This salad is a delicious alternative to a mixed green salad, and could form the basis of a light luncheon when served with fresh, hot biscuits.

PREPARATION TIME: 15 minutes

COOKING TIME: 40 minutes

SERVES: 8

INGREDIENTS

☐ 30oz fresh or frozen butter beans   ☐ 4 cups water
☐ 1 tsp salt   ☐ 4 hard-boiled eggs, chopped
☐ 1 small onion, finely grated   ☐ 1 cup mayonnaise
☐ ¾ tsp prepared mustard   ☐ ¾ tsp Worcestershire sauce
☐ ¾ tsp hot sauce

Boil the butter beans in the water and salt for 40 minutes. Drain, then combine with the rest of the ingredients. Refrigerate the salad overnight and serve on a bed of lettuce.

STURDIVANT MUSEUM ASSOCIATION,
SELMA, AL

Above: Butter Bean Salad.

SOUTHERN FRIED CHICKEN

This is one way to cook that real Southern Fried Chicken!

PREPARATION TIME: 15 minutes

COOKING TIME: 30 minutes

SERVES: 4

INGREDIENTS

- ☐ 1 chicken, fresh or killed the day before
- ☐ Flour for dredging ☐ Salt and pepper to taste

Cut the chicken into portions and wipe dry. Dredge in flour which has been seasoned with salt and pepper. Fry in boiling oil in a skillet. Cook only a few pieces at a time.

STURDIVANT MUSEUM ASSOCIATION,
SELMA, AL

Above: no Southern cookbook would be complete without a recipe for Fried Chicken.

ALABAMA COLA GLAZED HAM

Don't be afraid to try this somewhat unusual approach to roast ham. Cola gives it a marvelous taste and color.

PREPARATION TIME: 30 minutes, plus overnight soaking

COOKING TIME: 2¼ hours

SERVES: 8-10

--- INGREDIENTS ---

☐ 10lb joint country or Smithfield ham ☐ 4 cups cola soft drink
☐ Whole cloves ☐ 1 cup packed dark brown sugar

Soak the ham overnight. Preheat oven to 350°F. Place the ham rind side down in a roasting pan. Pour over all but 6 tbsps of the cola and bake, uncovered, 1½ hours or until the internal temperature registers 140°F. Baste the ham every 20 minutes with pan juices using a large spoon or a bulb baster. Remove the ham from the oven and allow it to cool for 10-15 minutes. Remove the rind from the ham with a small, sharp knife and score the fat to a depth of ¼ inch. Stick 1 clove in the center of every other diamond. Mix sugar and the remaining cola together and pour or spread over the ham. Raise the oven temperature to 375°F. Return the ham to the oven and bake for 45 minutes, basting every 15 minutes. Cover loosely with foil if the ham begins to brown too much. Allow to stand 15 minutes before slicing.

Above: Alabama Cola Glazed Ham. Facing page: the beautifully preserved first Confederate White House in Montgomery.

MARINATED PORK LOIN WITH ORANGE SAUCE

The orange adds a refreshing tang to a succulent pork roast.

PREPARATION TIME: 30 minutes
COOKING TIME: 2½ hours
SERVES: 8

INGREDIENTS

- □ 5lb loin of pork or
- □ 8 pork chops, 1 inch thick

MARINADE

- □ ½ cup lemon juice
- □ ½ cup soy sauce
- □ ½ cup red wine
- □ ½ tsp pressed garlic
- □ 2 tsps ground ginger

ORANGE SAUCE

- □ ⅔ cup sugar
- □ ½ tsp cinnamon
- □ 1 tbsp grated orange rind
- □ 20 whole cloves, tied in a cheesecloth bag
- □ 1 tbsp cornstarch
- □ ½ tsp salt
- □ 1 cup orange juice
- □ 8 orange slices, cut into halves

Combine the marinade ingredients and pour over the pork. Cover and refrigerate overnight, turning occasionally. Remove the meat, reserving the marinade for basting. Roast at 350°F, basting often with the reserved marinade, for approximately 2½ hours, or until the meat registers 185°F on a meat thermometer. To prepare the orange sauce, combine the sugar, spices, orange rind, orange juice, cornstarch and salt in a saucepan and cook over a medium heat, stirring frequently, until the sauce is thickened and clear. Remove the bag of cloves and add the orange slices.

To serve, arrange the meat on a serving platter and pour the orange sauce over the meat.

STURDIVANT MUSEUM ASSOCIATION,
SELMA, AL

Facing page: Marinated Pork Loin with Orange Sauce is set out in the grounds of one of Alabama's white-columned mansions.

JEFFERSON DAVIS PUNCH

This festive punch was especially created by the Davis family to celebrate a family birthday.

PREPARATION TIME: 15 minutes

YIELD: 200 cups of punch

INGREDIENTS

- □ 1½ pints lemon juice
- □ 3½ lbs sugar dissolved in water
- □ 12 bottles claret
- □ 2 bottles light rum
- □ 2 bottles dry sherry
- □ 1 bottle ginger ale
- □ 6 bottles club soda

GARNISH

- □ Ice
- □ Cucumber slices
- □ Orange slices

Combine all the ingredients in a large punch bowl. Dilute with water to taste. Float ice, cucumber and orange slices on top.

DAVIS FAMILY

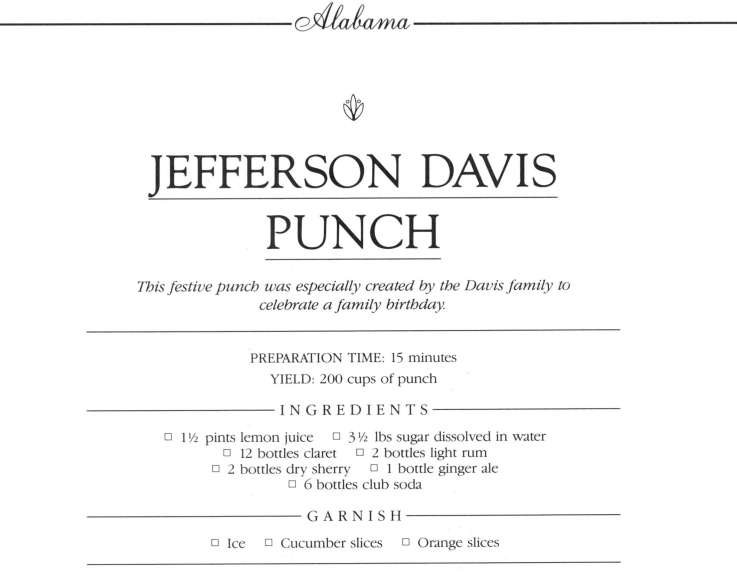

Above: Jefferson Davis Punch and Toasted Pecans.

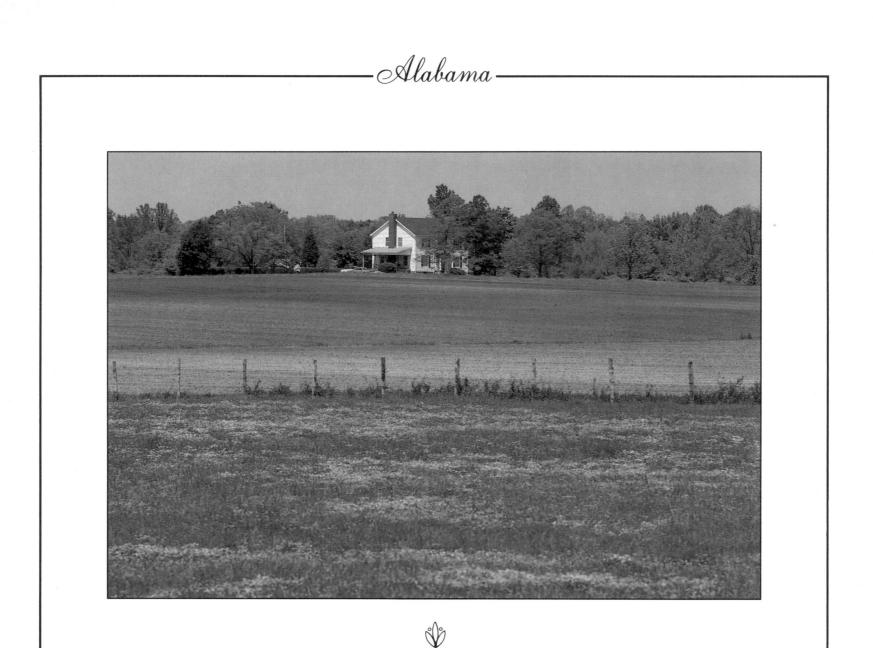

TOASTED PECANS

These nuts are wonderful served slightly warm on a cold night. They also freeze well for another time.

PREPARATION TIME: 10 minutes
COOKING TIME: 10 minutes
YIELD: 1lb

INGREDIENTS

☐ 1lb pecan halves, shelled   ☐ ½ stick (2oz) butter
☐ Salt to taste

Preheat the oven to 350°F. Melt the butter in a saucepan and add the pecans. Toss with a wooden spoon over a high heat until the butter has been absorbed. Spread the pecans on a cookie sheet and bake for approximately 10 minutes. Watch carefully because the nuts burn easily. When the pecans are bubbly and toasted, remove from the oven and immediately spread them on layers of absorbent paper towels. Sprinkle with salt while still hot. Cool before storing.

MRS. JOHN H. NAPIER III,
HAMNER GARLAND FREEMAN Jr.

Above: a weatherboarded farmstead is sheltered by trees in the farmland near Courtland.

BIG MOMMY'S
FLOATING ISLAND

Use your imagination to vary the flavorings in this spectacular dessert.

PREPARATION TIME: 30 minutes
COOKING TIME: 20-25 minutes
SERVES: 8-10

INGREDIENTS

CUSTARD

☐ 2 cups whole milk   ☐ 3 egg yolks or 2 whole eggs
☐ ¼ cup sugar   ☐ ½ tsp vanilla   ☐ ⅛ tsp salt
☐ A flavoring, such as nutmeg, amaretto or grated orange or lemon peel

"ISLANDS"

☐ 3 egg whites   ☐ 1 tsp cream of tartar   ☐ 1 tbsp sugar

To prepare the custard, scald the milk. Beat the eggs lightly and add the sugar and salt. Add this mixture to the hot milk, stirring constantly. Cook in the top of a double boiler, stirring often, until the mixture thickens and coats the back of the spoon. Cool and flavor using the flavoring of your choice. Chill the custard while you prepare the "Islands". Beat the egg whites and cream of tartar until stiff and gradually beat in the sugar to make a meringue with stiff peaks. Using a large tablespoon, float the meringues onto a roasting pan filled with hot milk or water. Brown in a preheated 400°F oven. Remove from the pan and drain.

To assemble the dessert, pour the chilled custard into a serving bowl. Using a slotted spoon, arrange the drained meringues on top.

MRS. JOHN H. NAPIER III

CHARLOTTE

This elegant and delicious dessert will grace any dinner party table.

PREPARATION TIME: 30 minutes

COOKING TIME: approximately 10 minutes

SERVES: 8-10

INGREDIENTS

□ 2 tbsps unflavored gelatin   □ ¼ cup cold water
□ 2 cups milk   □ 4 eggs, separated
□ ½ cup sugar   □ ⅛ tsp salt
□ 2 tbsps whiskey   □ 1 pint whipping cream
□ 1 dozen lady fingers

In a mixing bowl, sprinkle the gelatin over the cold water and leave to soak until all of the gelatin is moist. Heat the milk to just below boiling and set aside to cool slightly. Meanwhile, separate the eggs and beat the yolks slightly. Add the sugar and salt, followed by a small amount of the hot milk. Stir well. Add this mixture to the remaining hot milk and cook over a low heat, stirring constantly, until the mixture coats the back of the spoon. Pour this mixture over the gelatin in the mixing bowl and stir until the gelatin is dissolved. Cool, then add the whiskey. When the mixture begins to gel, beat the egg whites until stiff, but still moist. Fold the egg whites into the custard by cutting a spoon through the egg whites and custard and turning the custard over the egg whites. Blend in this manner until no lumps of egg white are visible. Beat the cream until stiff and fold into the mixture in the same way as the egg whites. Line a mold with lady fingers and spoon the custard mixture on top. Cover and chill thoroughly.

To serve, unmold and top with additional whipped cream.

STURDIVANT MUSEUM ASSOCIATION,
SELMA, AL

Above: Charlotte and (previous pages) Big Mommy's Floating Island are two French influenced desserts.

Flavor of
MISSISSIPPI

OLD SOUTH TURNIP GREENS AND POT LIQUOR

Here is real down home cooking at its best!

PREPARATION TIME: 30 minutes

COOKING TIME: 2 hours

SERVES: 8

INGREDIENTS

- 2lbs salt pork
- 8 cups cold water
- 1 tsp crushed red pepper
- 2 tsps salt
- ½ tsp pepper
- 6lbs young, tender turnip greens, washed several times

TO SERVE

- Sliced hard-boiled eggs
- Sliced green onions
- Pot liquor

In a large pot, combine the salt pork, water, red pepper, salt and pepper. Bring to a boil, then reduce the heat, cover and cook slowly for 1 hour. Add the well washed turnip greens and cook, covered, over a low heat for a further hour, or until the greens and pork are tender. To serve, remove the turnip greens from the pot. Chop them and arrange them in a large serving dish. Place the pork on top and garnish with slices of hard-boiled egg and green onions. Pour the pot liquor over the dish before serving.

ANN HALL, GREY OAKS,
VICKSBURG, MS

Previous pages: the Sandbar, Great River Road Park. Above: Old South Turnip Greens and Pot Liquor. Facing page: a derelict church at Grand Gulf.

CRISPY FRIED
CATFISH

PREPARATION TIME: 45 minutes
COOKING TIME: 10-15 minutes
SERVES: 6

INGREDIENTS

□ 6 catfish □ ½ cup evaporated milk □ 1 tbsp salt
□ Dash pepper □ 1 egg □ 1 cup flour □ ½ cup yellow cornmeal
□ 2 tsps paprika □ Oil or lard for frying

Clean, skin, wash and dry the catfish before cutting them into serving-sized portions. Beat the egg into the milk and stir in the salt and pepper. In a separate bowl, combine the flour, cornmeal and paprika. Dip the cleaned fish in the milk mixture, then roll in the seasoned flour. Heat the oil or lard to 375°F on a fat thermometer, or until a 1-inch cube of bread turns golden after 1 minute, in a heavy-bottomed pan. When the oil is hot enough, add the fish and brown well on both sides. When the fish are well browned, lift them carefully from the pan and drain them on absorbent paper. Serve very hot.

Some cooks prefer to soak the catfish in buttermilk for several hours before frying.

ANN HALL, GREY OAKS,
VICKSBURG, MS

*Facing page: Crispy Fried Catfish tastes even more delicious when the fish have
been freshly caught in the Mississippi River (above).*

HUSH PUPPIES

Hush Puppies were originally made out of leftover corn bread batter. Serve them with meat and chicken.

PREPARATION TIME: 20 minutes
COOKING TIME: 10 minutes
YIELD: approximately 24 Hush Puppies

INGREDIENTS

☐ 1 egg, well beaten   ☐ ⅔ cup milk   ☐ 1½ cups white cornmeal
☐ ½ cup flour, sifted   ☐ ½ tsp sugar   ☐ 1 tsp baking powder
☐ ½ tsp salt   ☐ 1 bunch (approximately 1 cup) fresh green onions, finely chopped
☐ Pinch red pepper   ☐ Pinch garlic powder   ☐ Oil for deep-fat frying

Mix together the eggs, milk, cornmeal, flour, sugar, baking powder and salt until well blended and smooth. Add the green onions, red pepper and garlic powder. Shape the dough into small balls. If the dough is too soft, add more cornmeal. Fry the Hush Puppies in deep fat which has been heated to 360°F until they are browned. Drain on absorbent paper.

ANN HALL, GREY OAKS,
VICKSBURG, MS

Above and facing page: these landscapes are everyone's idea of true Mississippi country.

BREASTS OF CHICKEN VICKSBURG

This delicious chicken is sure to be as popular with your guests as it is with the guests at the Magnolia Inn in Vicksburg

PREPARATION TIME: 30 minutes

COOKING TIME: 45 minutes

SERVES: 6

INGREDIENTS

□ 6 chicken breasts, split and skinned   □ ¼ cup flour   □ 2 ½ tsps salt
□ 1 tsp paprika   □ ½ cup butter   □ ¼ cup water   □ 2 tsps cornstarch
□ 1½ cups half and half or light cream   □ ¼ cup sherry
□ 1 cup mushrooms, sliced   □ 1 cup Swiss cheese, grated
□ ½ cup fresh parsley, chopped

TO SERVE

□ 6 slices of bread, toasted and with the crusts removed
□ 6 thin slices of cooked ham

Above: Breasts of Chicken Vicksburg.

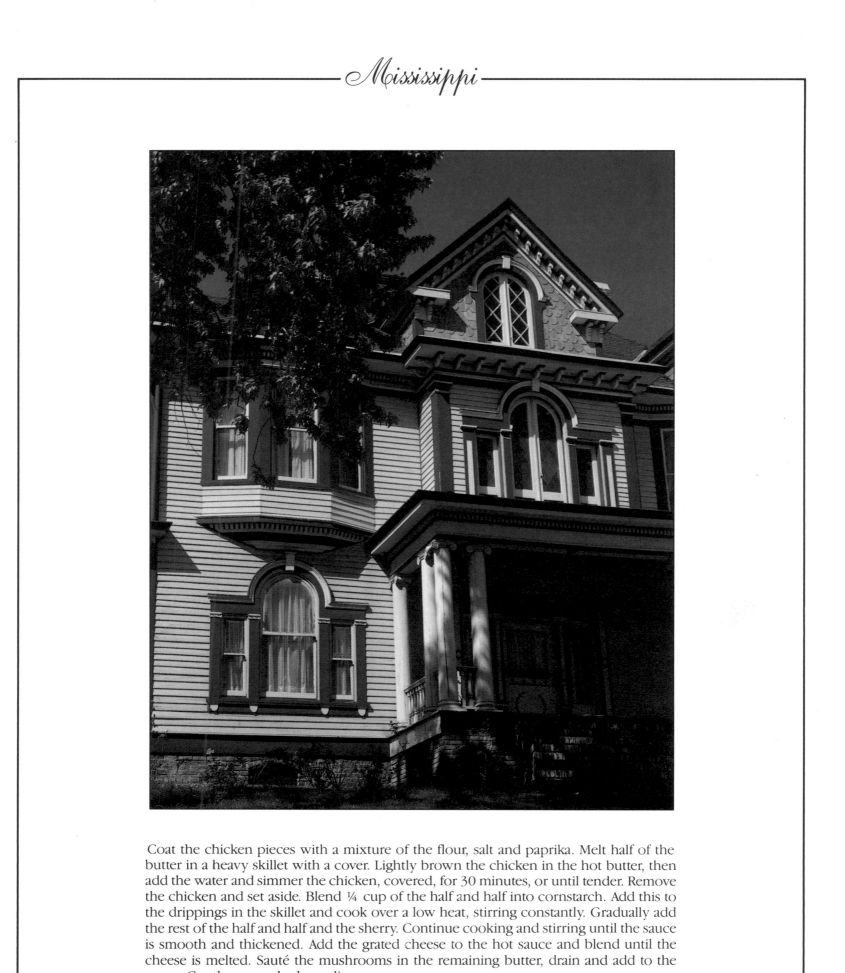

Coat the chicken pieces with a mixture of the flour, salt and paprika. Melt half of the butter in a heavy skillet with a cover. Lightly brown the chicken in the hot butter, then add the water and simmer the chicken, covered, for 30 minutes, or until tender. Remove the chicken and set aside. Blend ¼ cup of the half and half into cornstarch. Add this to the drippings in the skillet and cook over a low heat, stirring constantly. Gradually add the rest of the half and half and the sherry. Continue cooking and stirring until the sauce is smooth and thickened. Add the grated cheese to the hot sauce and blend until the cheese is melted. Sauté the mushrooms in the remaining butter, drain and add to the sauce. Gently warm the ham slices.

To serve, place the pieces of toast on a large, oblong platter. Top each with a slice of warm ham, then a chicken breast. Cover each serving with the hot sauce. Garnish with chopped parsley and paprika. The serving may also be arranged separately in small individual casserole dishes.

MARTIN LAFFEY,
DELTA POINT RIVER RESTAURANT,
VICKSBURG, MS

Above: built in 1901, this house is a fine example of decorative Southern architecture.

ORANGE-GLAZED
SOUTHERN HENS

This makes a very special dinner for 2.

PREPARATION TIME: 30-45 minutes

COOKING TIME: 1 hour

SERVES: 2

INGREDIENTS

☐ Cornish hen (1-1½ lbs) ☐ ¼ cup butter
☐ 1 6oz package long-grain and wild rice mix
☐ 1 4oz can chopped mushrooms, drained
☐ ¼ cup orange peel, cut into julienne strips ☐ 3½ tbsps light brown sugar
☐ 2¼ tbsps cornstarch ☐ ⅔ cup water ☐ ¾ cup orange juice
☐ ¼ tsp salt ☐ 1½ tbsps brandy

Rinse the hen and pat dry. Brush with butter and salt and bake at 350°F for 1 hour, brushing occasionally with more butter. Meanwhile, cook the rice according to the package directions. When the rice is cooked, stir in the mushrooms and heat through. Set aside to keep warm while you prepare the sauce.

First, simmer the orange peel in a small amount of water in a covered saucepan for 15 minutes. Drain well and set aside. In another saucepan, combine the brown sugar and cornstarch. Blend in the water and orange juice and cook and stir over a low heat until the sauce is thickened, about 2-3 minutes. Remove from the heat and stir in the orange peel and brandy. Arrange the hen on a serving platter and spoon the sauce on top. Serve with the rice.

CARL ANDRÉ FLOWERS,
CEDAR GROVE ESTATE, VICKSBURG, MS

*Facing page: Orange-Glazed Southern Hens. Above: the bridges spanning the
Mississippi River are impressive feats of engineering.*

BOURBON RIBS

Try these for one of the best barbecues you have ever tasted.

PREPARATION TIME: 20 minutes
COOKING TIME: 55 minutes, plus 45 minutes grilling on a barbecue
SERVES: 6

INGREDIENTS

☐ 4lbs beef or pork ribs

SAUCE

☐ 1 medium onion, chopped (approximately ½ cup)   ☐ ½ cup light molasses
☐ ½ cup catsup   ☐ 2 tsps orange peel, finely shredded   ☐ ⅓ cup orange juice
☐ 2 tbsps cooking oil   ☐ 1 tbsp vinegar   ☐ 1 tbsp steak sauce
☐ ½ tsp prepared mustard   ☐ ½ tsp Worcestershire sauce
☐ ¼ tsp garlic powder   ☐ ¼ tsp salt   ☐ ¼ tsp pepper
☐ ¼ tsp hot pepper sauce   ☐ ⅛ tsp ground cloves   ☐ ¼ cup bourbon

Place the ribs in a large Dutch oven or saucepan and add water to cover. Bring to the boil, then reduce the heat and simmer, covered, for 40-55 minutes or until the ribs are tender. Remove from the heat and drain thoroughly. While the ribs are cooking, prepare the sauce by combining all of the sauce ingredients in a pan. Bring the mixture to the boil and simmer gently, uncovered, for 15 to 20 minutes.

When the ribs are tender and the sauce is prepared, grill the ribs over slow coals on a barbecue for about 45 minutes. Turn every 15 minutes and baste with the sauce. Extra sauce can be served with the meat.

CARL ANDRÉ FLOWERS,
CEDAR GROVE ESTATE, VICKSBURG, MS

*Above: Glen Auburn, one of the gracious antebellum houses in Natchez.
Facing page: Bourbon Ribs.*

JEFFERSON DAVIS PIE

Named in honor of one of the heroes of the Confederacy, this pie is sure to please.

PREPARATION TIME: 20 minutes

COOKING TIME: 50-60 minutes

SERVES: 8

INGREDIENTS

□ 1 tbsp flour   □ 1 tbsp cornmeal   □ 2 cups sugar   □ 4 eggs
□ ¼ cup butter, melted   □ ¼ cup lemon juice   □ 1 tbsp grated lemon rind
□ ¼ cup milk   □ 1 9-inch unbaked pie shell

Sift the flour and cornmeal into the sugar. Beat the eggs slightly and add to the sugar mixture, blending well. Add the butter, lemon juice, lemon rind and milk. Pour this filling into the unbaked pie shell. Bake at 350°F for 50-60 minutes or until the filling is set and the center is firm.

MARTIN LAFFEY,
DELTA POINT RIVER RESTAURANT,
VICKSBURG, MS

Previous pages: Jefferson Davis Pie.
Above: the National Historic Landmark of Longwood, Natchez.

CHERRIES JUBILEE

This spectacular dessert is really simple to make, and delicious to eat!

PREPARATION TIME: 15 minutes

COOKING TIME: 5-10 minutes, plus flaming

SERVES: 4-6

INGREDIENTS

☐ 1 17oz can pitted fancy Oregon Bing cherries ☐ 4 tbsps butter
☐ ¼ cup sugar ☐ 1 tbsp cornstarch ☐ ¼ cup brandy

TO SERVE

☐ Vanilla ice cream

In a bowl, stir ½ cup of the cherry juice into the cornstarch and set aside. Melt the butter and sugar in a heavy skillet over a low heat. Add the cherries and the rest of the juice to the skillet and stir to coat, then blend in the cornstarch mixture. Cook and stir over low heat until thickened. Place the mixture in a warm chafing dish. When ready to serve, pour the brandy over the cherries and ignite. When the flames die down, serve over vanilla ice cream.

CRAIG R. GIBSON,
CEDAR GROVE ESTATE, VICKSBURG, MS

Above: Cherries Jubilee.

BOURBON PIE

This pie looks as elegant as it tastes!

PREPARATION TIME: 45 minutes, plus 1-2 hours chilling
COOKING TIME: approximately 20 minutes
SERVES: 8

INGREDIENTS

CHOCOLATE CRUST

☐ 1½ cups chocolate wafer crumbs
☐ 1 tbsp sugar   ☐ 4 tbsps unsalted butter or margarine, melted

PIE FILLING

☐ 21 large marshmallows   ☐ 1 cup evaporated milk   ☐ 1 cup whipping cream
☐ 3 tbsps bourbon   ☐ ½ cup chopped pecans (optional)

Above: restored in the 1960s, Waverly, near West Point, was originally built in 1852.

TOPPING

☐ 1 cup whipping cream ☐ 2 tbsps powdered sugar
☐ 1½ tsps vanilla extract ☐ 2-3oz semi-sweet chocolate, grated

First prepare the crust by tossing all ingredients together until the crumbs are moist. Pat the mixture into the bottom and sides of a 9-inch pie pan. Bake in an oven, preheated to 350°F, for 10-12 minutes. Cool, then cover and refrigerate until needed.

To make the filling, combine the marshmallows and the evaporated milk in a heavy 3-quart saucepan or double boiler and cook over medium heat until the marshmallows melt, stirring often. Be careful not to allow the mixture to boil. Cover and refrigerate for approximately 1-2 hours. When the marshmallow mixture is chilled, whip the cream and the bourbon together until stiff peaks form. Fold into the chilled marshmallow mixture along with the pecans, if used. Pour the filling into the prepared crust, smooth the top and chill until set, about 4-5 hours.

Before serving, prepare the topping. With an electric mixer, beat all the topping ingredients together, except for the grated chocolate, until stiff peaks form. Spread over the chilled and set pie. Garnish with the grated chocolate.

HELEN MARIE ABRAHAM,
CEDAR GROVE ESTATE, VICKSBURG, MS

Above: Bourbon Pie.

Flavor of
LOUISIANA

SHRIMP BISQUE

This classic Cajun recipe makes a first course or a full meal.
It isn't a smooth purée like its French counterpart.

PREPARATION TIME: 20 minutes

COOKING TIME: 8-10 minutes

SERVES: 6

INGREDIENTS

☐ 3 tbsps butter or margarine ☐ 1 onion, finely chopped
☐ 1 red pepper, seeded and finely chopped ☐ 2 sticks celery, finely chopped
☐ 1 clove garlic, minced ☐ Pinch dry mustard and cayenne pepper
☐ 2 tsps paprika ☐ 3 tbsps flour ☐ 4 cups fish stock
☐ 1 sprig thyme and bay leaf ☐ 8oz raw, peeled shrimp
☐ Salt and pepper ☐ Snipped chives

Melt the butter or margarine and add the onion, pepper, celery and garlic. Cook gently to soften. Stir in the mustard, cayenne, paprika and flour. Cook about 3 minutes over gentle heat, stirring occasionally. Pour on the stock gradually, stirring until well blended. Add the thyme and bay leaf and bring to the boil. Reduce the heat and simmer about 5 minutes or until thickened, stirring occasionally. Add the shrimp and cook until pink and curled, about 5 minutes. Season with salt and pepper to taste and top with snipped chives before serving.

Previous pages: St. Gabriel's Church, Mississippi Valley. Facing page: Shrimp Bisque. Above: the delicate wrought iron balcony of Soniat House is typical of houses in the Vieux Carré, New Orleans.

NEW ORLEANS

JAMBALAYA

An easy and extremely satisfying dish of rice and seafood. Sometimes garlic sausage is added for extra spice.

PREPARATION TIME: 40 minutes

COOKING TIME: 25-30 minutes

SERVES: 4-6

INGREDIENTS

□ 2 tbsps butter or margarine □ 2 tbsps flour
□ 1 medium onion, finely chopped □ 1 clove garlic, crushed
□ 1 red pepper, seeded and finely chopped
□ 14oz canned tomatoes □ 4 cups fish or chicken stock
□ ¼ tsp ground ginger □ Pinch allspice
□ 1 tsp chopped fresh thyme or ½ tsp dried thyme
□ ¼ tsp cayenne pepper □ Pinch salt
□ Dash tabasco □ 4oz uncooked rice
□ 2lbs uncooked shrimp, peeled □ 2 green onions, chopped to garnish

Melt the butter in a heavy-based saucepan and then add the flour. Stir to blend well and cook over low heat until a pale straw color. Add the onion, garlic and pepper and cook until soft. Add the tomatoes and their juice, breaking up the tomatoes with a fork or a potato masher. Add the stock and mix well. Add the ginger, allspice, thyme, cayenne pepper, salt and tabasco. Bring to the boil and allow to boil rapidly, stirring for about 2 minutes. Add the rice, stir well and cover the pan. Cook for about 15-20 minutes, or until the rice is tender and has absorbed most of the liquid. Add the shrimp during the last 10 minutes of cooking time. Cook until the shrimp curl and turn pink. Adjust the seasoning, spoon into a serving dish and sprinkle with the chopped green onion to serve.

Above: New Orleans Jambalaya is a Creole dish that's as much of a tradition as steamers on the Mississippi River (facing page).

OYSTERS
JEAN LAFITTE

You can really put your culinary skills to the test with this fine example of the French influence on Louisiana Cajun cuisine.

PREPARATION TIME: 1 hour

COOKING TIME: 20 minutes

SERVES: 4

INGREDIENTS

OYSTERS

- □ 12 select oysters
- □ 1 cup milk
- □ 1 small egg
- □ 3 tsps salt
- □ ½ tsp black pepper
- □ ½ tsp white pepper
- □ ½ tsp cayenne pepper
- □ ½ tsp granulated garlic
- □ 1 cup cornmeal
- □ Oil for deep fat frying

CROUTONS

- □ 12 slices French bread
- □ ¼ cup butter, melted
- □ 1 tsp. granulated garlic

BROWN MEUNIÈRE SAUCE

- □ ¼ cup prepared Demi-Glace (see recipe)
- □ ¼ cup dry white wine
- □ 1oz lemon juice
- □ ½ lb cold, unsalted butter
- □ Salt and cayenne pepper to taste

Begin by preparing the oysters. Beat the egg and combine with the milk and half of each of the seasonings. Soak the oysters in the milk. Meanwhile, combine the rest of the seasonings with the cornmeal. Take the oysters from the milk, allowing excess liquid to drain off, and dredge them in the seasoned cornmeal. Fry in deep fat, heated to 375°F, for 5-7 minutes depending on size or until golden brown. Drain on absorbent paper. Keep warm while you prepare the rest of the dish.

To prepare the croutons, brush the bread with melted butter. Sprinkle on the granulated garlic and toast in a 400°F oven until light brown. Keep warm while you make the meunière sauce.

In a saucepan, combine the previously prepared demi-glace, wine and lemon juice. Reduce over a medium-high heat to approximately 4 ounces in volume. Cut the butter into ½-inch pieces. Add to the saucepan 3 pieces at a time, stirring constantly with a wire whisk. When all the butter has been incorporated, remove the sauce from the heat. Season to taste with salt and cayenne pepper.

While the sauce is warm, assemble the dish. Arrange the croutons on a plate and top with the fried oysters. Cover the oysters with some of the brown meunière sauce and serve immediately. Extra sauce can be served separately using an empty oyster shell as a dish.

JOHN D. FOLSE, LAFITTE'S LANDING,
P.O. BOX 1128, DONALDSONVILLE, LA

Facing page: Oysters Jean Lafitte.

FROG LEGS

PREPARATION TIME: 15 minutes

COOKING TIME: 15 minutes

SERVES: 4

──────── INGREDIENTS ────────

☐ ½ cup butter   ☐ 4 tbsps olive oil
☐ 6 cloves garlic, minced   ☐ 1 tbsp cracked black peppercorns
☐ ¼ cup scallions, chopped   ☐ 8 frog legs, approximately 4 inches long
☐ 1oz white wine   ☐ 1 tbsp chopped pimentoes
☐ ¼ cup parsley, chopped   ☐ ½ tsp cayenne pepper
☐ 1 tsp salt

──────── GARNISH ────────

☐ 4 lemon slices   ☐ 4 sprigs parsley

Melt the butter in a heavy-bottomed sauté pan over a medium-high heat. Add the olive oil, garlic, peppercorns and scallions. Sauté for 1 minute, stirring constantly to prevent the garlic from browning. Add the frog legs and continue to stir and cook until they are opaque in appearance and tender to the touch, approximately 3 minutes. Deglaze with the white wine, then add the pimentoes, parsley, salt and cayenne pepper. Serve the frog legs with the sauce from the pan, garnished with lemon slices and parsley sprigs.

These delicious frog legs are also good served with a Bordelaise sauce.

JOHN D. FOLSE, LAFITTE'S LANDING,
P.O. BOX 1128, DONALDSONVILLE, LA

Above: Frog Legs, a French influenced dish using one local ingredient readily available in the Louisiana swamps and bayous, (facing page)!

STUFFED EGGPLANT
WITH SHRIMP

PREPARATION TIME: 45 minutes

COOKING TIME: 1 hour

SERVES: 8

──────── INGREDIENTS ────────

☐ 4 medium eggplants   ☐ 2 tbsps shortening
☐ 1 cup chopped onions   ☐ 1 cup chopped bell pepper
☐ ½ cup chopped celery   ☐ 2 cloves garlic, chopped
☐ ½ cup chopped scallions   ☐ 1lb ground beef
☐ 1lb fresh shrimp, chopped   ☐ 3 ½ cups seasoned Italian bread crumbs
☐ 2 eggs, beaten   ☐ Salt and pepper to taste

Slice the eggplants lengthwise and place in a pot of lightly salted water. Bring to a rolling boil and cook until tender. Drain, cool and scoop out the flesh, being careful not to tear the shell. Drain the excess water from the flesh and chop finely.

Melt the shortening in a sauté pan over a medium high heat. Sauté the onions, scallions, bell pepper, garlic and celery for approximately five minutes, stirring occasionally. Add the ground beef and blend well into the vegetable mixture. Continue cooking for approximately 20 minutes or until brown. Finally, add the shrimp and chopped eggplant flesh. Cook for about 30 minutes, stirring occasionally to keep from sticking. Add 2 ½ cups of the seasoned bread crumbs and the beaten eggs and mix well. Season to taste with salt and cayenne pepper. Use this mixture to stuff the eggplant shells. Top with the remaining bread crumbs. Bake at 350°F for 5-10 minutes, or until brown.

The shrimp add a Louisiana flavor to these stuffed eggplants. You can also serve the filling in a casserole if you don't wish to stuff the eggplant shells.

JOHN D. FOLSE, LAFITTE'S LANDING,
P.O. BOX 1128, DONALDSONVILLE, LA

Above: Lafitte's blacksmith shop in New Orleans.
Facing page: Stuffed Eggplant with Shrimp.

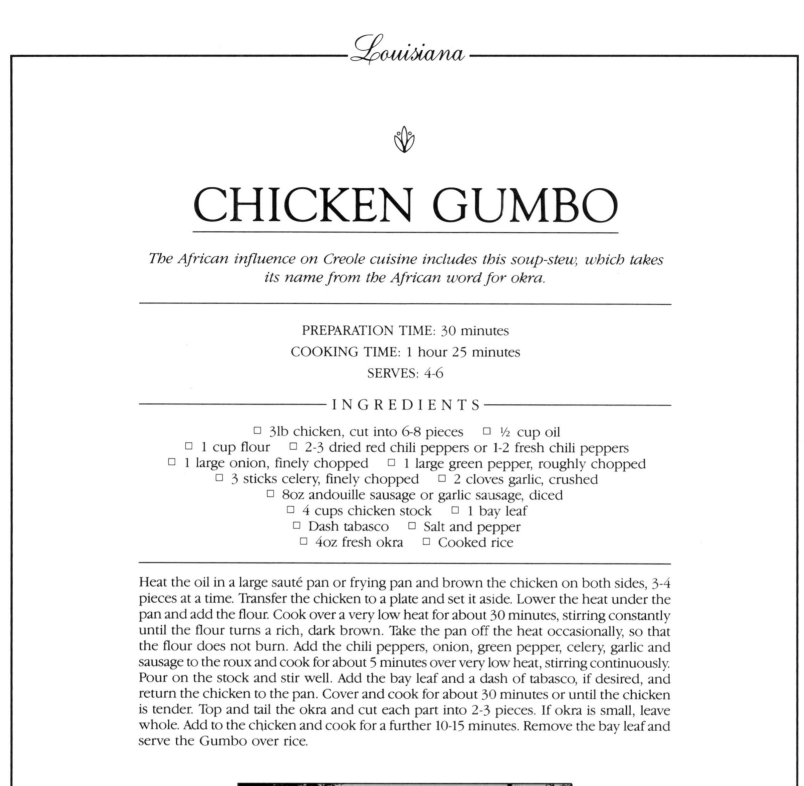

CHICKEN GUMBO

*The African influence on Creole cuisine includes this soup-stew, which takes
its name from the African word for okra.*

PREPARATION TIME: 30 minutes

COOKING TIME: 1 hour 25 minutes

SERVES: 4-6

INGREDIENTS

☐ 3lb chicken, cut into 6-8 pieces ☐ ½ cup oil
☐ 1 cup flour ☐ 2-3 dried red chili peppers or 1-2 fresh chili peppers
☐ 1 large onion, finely chopped ☐ 1 large green pepper, roughly chopped
☐ 3 sticks celery, finely chopped ☐ 2 cloves garlic, crushed
☐ 8oz andouille sausage or garlic sausage, diced
☐ 4 cups chicken stock ☐ 1 bay leaf
☐ Dash tabasco ☐ Salt and pepper
☐ 4oz fresh okra ☐ Cooked rice

Heat the oil in a large sauté pan or frying pan and brown the chicken on both sides, 3-4
pieces at a time. Transfer the chicken to a plate and set it aside. Lower the heat under the
pan and add the flour. Cook over a very low heat for about 30 minutes, stirring constantly
until the flour turns a rich, dark brown. Take the pan off the heat occasionally, so that
the flour does not burn. Add the chili peppers, onion, green pepper, celery, garlic and
sausage to the roux and cook for about 5 minutes over very low heat, stirring continuously.
Pour on the stock and stir well. Add the bay leaf and a dash of tabasco, if desired, and
return the chicken to the pan. Cover and cook for about 30 minutes or until the chicken
is tender. Top and tail the okra and cut each part into 2-3 pieces. If okra is small, leave
whole. Add to the chicken and cook for a further 10-15 minutes. Remove the bay leaf and
serve the Gumbo over rice.

*Facing page: Chicken Gumbo. Above: Oakley House, St. Francisville, to which
John James Audubon, author of* The Birds of America *came in 1821 as tutor to
the owner's daughter.*

CAJUN STUFFED FILET MIGNON

Seafood and beef are combined in this recipe to make a very elegant dinner for two.

PREPARATION TIME: 40 minutes

COOKING TIME: 30 minutes

SERVES: 2

INGREDIENTS

☐ 2 9oz filet mignons   ☐ ¼ cup melted butter
☐ 1 tbsp crushed thyme   ☐ 1 tbsp tarragon
☐ 1 tbsp sweet basil   ☐ 1 tbsp rosemary
☐ Salt and cayenne pepper to taste   ☐ ¾ cup dry red wine

Above: a double layer of iron tracery encases the facade of this Vieux Carré building in New Orleans.

WHITE SAUCE

- ½ cup milk
- 1 bay leaf
- 1 slice onion
- 3 peppercorns
- 1 tbsp butter
- 1 tbsp flour
- Salt and pepper to taste

CAJUN CRAB MEAT STUFFING

- ¾ lb white crab meat
- ¼ cup diced onions
- ¼ cup diced celery
- ¼ cup pimentos
- 2 cloves garlic, chopped
- ¼ cup scallions, chopped
- ½ tsp Dijon mustard
- ½ tsp Pernod
- 1 tbsp sherry
- 1 tbsp fresh parsley, chopped
- Salt and cayenne pepper to taste

Trim the excess fat and cut a ¾-inch pocket in the center of each filet. Place the meat in a roasting pan and add the butter and herbs, making sure the herbs are well distributed over each filet. Season with salt and cayenne pepper.

Next prepare the white sauce. Combine the milk, bay leaf, onion slice and peppercorns in a saucepan and bring to the boil. Remove from the heat and leave to stand for 15 minutes. In a separate pan, melt the butter and stir in the flour to make a smooth paste. Cook briefly over a moderate heat, stirring constantly. Strain the milk and gradually add to the flour, stirring constantly. Bring to the boil and simmer until the sauce is thick enough to coat the back of a spoon. Set aside to add to the stuffing.

To prepare the stuffing, combine all of the ingredients and stir in the prepared white sauce. Stuff the pockets in the meat with this mixture. Roast at 475°F for approximately 15 minutes. Deglaze the roasting pan with ¾ cup of red wine, then reduce the volume by half. Serve as a sauce over the filets.

JOHN D. FOLSE, LAFITTE'S LANDING,
P.O. BOX 1128, DONALDSONVILLE, LA

Above: Cajun Stuffed Filet Mignon.

BEIGNETS

A night on the town in New Orleans is not complete without stopping for chicory coffee and fresh hot beignets.

PREPARATION TIME: 1 hour

COOKING TIME: 15 minutes

YIELD: 20 beignets

INGREDIENTS

- ½ cup milk, warmed to blood temperature
- 2 tsps dried yeast or ⅓ oz fresh yeast
- 1 egg, beaten
- ⅛ cup sugar
- ½ tsp salt
- 1¾ cups bread flour
- ⅛ cup butter, softened
- Oil for deep fat frying
- Confectioners' sugar

Dissolve the yeast in the warm milk, then add the sugar, salt and beaten egg. Gradually add half of the flour, stirring until well blended, then mix in the softened butter. Gradually add the rest of the flour until the dough is very stiff and can only be mixed with your hands.

Place the dough in a warm bowl and cover with a towel. Leave it to rise in a warm place for approximately 1 hour, or until it has doubled in bulk. Knead gently on a floured surface, then roll out to a ¼-inch thickness. Cut the dough into rectangles approximately 2½ x 3½ inches and place on a lightly floured pan. Cover with a towel and leave to rise for approximately 35 minutes. Deep fry in oil which has been heated to 360°F, turning once when the bottom side has browned. Drain on paper towels, then dust generously with confectioners' sugar.

JOHN D. FOLSE, LAFITTE'S LANDING,
P.O. BOX 1128, DONALDSONVILLE, LA

Facing page: Beignets.
Above: the real and the unreal figures of Mardi Gras are equally fantastic.

Flavor of
ARKANSAS

CATFISH
HORS D' OEUVRE

*These well spiced and crispy morsels are a favorite in the
Governor's Mansion.*

PREPARATION TIME: 20 minutes

COOKING TIME: 10–15 minutes

SERVES: 4–8

— INGREDIENTS —

☐ 4 catfish fillets, diced ☐ 1 cup yellow cornmeal
☐ ½ tsp garlic salt ☐ ½ tsp cayenne
☐ Oil for deep fat frying

Combine the cornmeal, garlic salt and cayenne pepper. Roll the diced catfish in this
mixture to coat. Deep fry in fat which has been heated to 375°F, or until a 1-inch cube
of bread browns in 1 minute. The fish pieces will sink to the bottom of the pan. When
they rise to the surface they are done. The pieces should be golden brown. Drain on
paper towels and serve hot.

LIZA, GOVERNOR'S MANSION,
LITTLE ROCK, AR

*Previous pages: Arkansas farmland north of Mountain View. Above: Catfish
Hors d'Oeuvre.*

PEPPERED HAM

This is the method used by Liza to prepare the hams which grace the table at the Governor's Mansion in Little Rock.

PREPARATION TIME: 15 minutes
COOKING TIME: 3½-4 hours
SERVES: 8-10

INGREDIENTS

☐ 1 fully cooked or cured ham   ☐ Liquid Smoke
☐ Sorghum molasses   ☐ Coarse ground pepper

Trim the excess fat off the ham and rub it with Liquid Smoke and sorghum molasses. Sprinkle generously with coarse ground pepper to cover. Wrap the ham in aluminum foil and refrigerate overnight. The next day, remove the foil and place the ham in a shallow roasting pan. Bake at 325°F for 3½ to 4 hours.

LIZA, GOVERNOR'S MANSION,
LITTLE ROCK, AR

Above: Peppered Ham.

TROUT ALMONDINE

Use the freshest trout you can find to make this simple, yet elegant dish.

PREPARATION TIME: 30 minutes

COOKING TIME: 10 minutes

SERVES: 2

INGREDIENTS

- ☐ 2 trout, cleaned and scaled
- ☐ 2 cups flour
- ☐ 1 tsp salt
- ☐ Pinch cayenne pepper
- ☐ 4oz (1 stick) butter
- ☐ Pinch dill
- ☐ Pinch thyme
- ☐ ¼ cup lemon juice
- ☐ 2oz sliced almonds
- ☐ 2 tbsps white wine

Season the flour with salt and cayenne. Roll the trout in the flour to coat. Melt the butter in a frying pan along with the dill and thyme. Sauté the trout in the butter for approximately 3 minutes, turn and continue cooking until the fish is done, about 3-4 minutes longer. When the trout is fully cooked add the lemon juice, white wine and almonds. Bring the liquid to a boil and simmer briefly. To serve, arrange the trout on a platter and pour the sauce on top.

GARY KETCHUM,
CREATIVE CULINARY SYSTEMS,
LITTLE ROCK, AR

Facing page: this wooded Arkansas landscape looks cool and inviting.
Above: Trout Almondine and Curried Okra.

CURRIED OKRA

Fried Okra is a popular and tasty vegetable side dish.

PREPARATION TIME: 20 minutes
COOKING TIME: 10-15 minutes
SERVES: 4-6

— INGREDIENTS —

☐ 1lb okra, trimmed and washed   ☐ 1½ cups cornmeal
☐ 1 tsp salt   ☐ ¼ tsp cayenne pepper
☐ Oil for frying

Wash and trim the okra, but do not dry. Combine the cornmeal and the seasonings. Roll the okra in the cornmeal until well coated. Fry in hot oil in a skillet until golden brown. Drain the okra on paper towels before serving.

GARY KETCHUM,
CREATIVE CULINARY SYSTEMS,
LITTLE ROCK, AR

Above: a soft, early evening landscape of gray and gold.
Facing page: built in 1832 but idle today, Pugh's Old Mill is situated at North Little Rock.

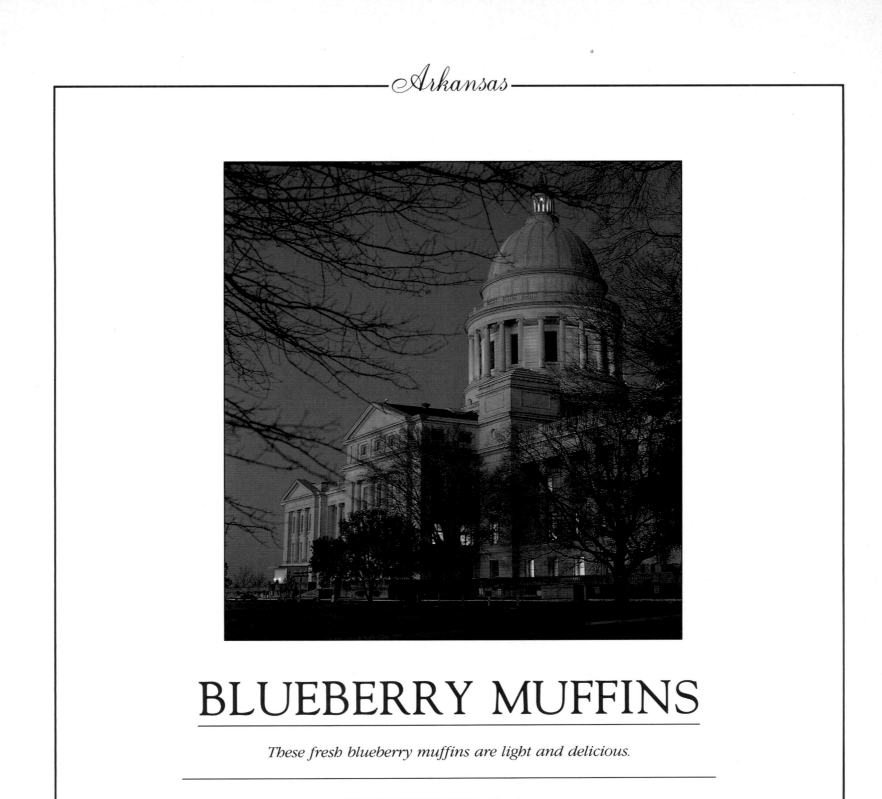

BLUEBERRY MUFFINS

These fresh blueberry muffins are light and delicious.

PREPARATION TIME: 15 minutes
COOKING TIME: 25 minutes
YIELD: approximately 2 dozen

INGREDIENTS

- ☐ 2 cups flour
- ☐ 4 tsps baking powder
- ☐ ⅓ cup sugar
- ☐ 4 tsps baking powder
- ☐ ½ tsp salt
- ☐ 1 cup fresh blueberries, washed and drained
- ☐ 1 egg, beaten
- ☐ ¼ cup margarine, melted
- ☐ 1 cup of milk

Sift together the dry ingredients and stir in the blueberries. Mix together the melted margarine, egg and milk. Stir this liquid mixture into the dry ingredients and mix just enough to moisten. Fill well greased muffin pans ¾ full. Bake at 400°F for 25 minutes, or until done.

GARY KETCHUM,
CREATIVE CULINARY SYSTEMS,
LITTLE ROCK, AR

Previous page: a mouthwatering selection of desserts.
Above: the Arkansas State Capitol building, Little Rock.

ASPBERRY ICE CREAM

This is a way to make delicious home-made ice cream without a special ice cream freezer.

PREPARATION TIME: 20 minutes
FREEZING TIME: approximately 3 hours
YIELD: approximately 1 quart

INGREDIENTS

□ 2 cups sweetened condensed milk
□ ½ cup water   □ 4 cups fresh raspberries
□ 4 tbsps lemon juice   □ 1 cup heavy cream

Combine the condensed milk, water, raspberries and lemon juice and refrigerate. Meanwhile, whip the cream in a chilled bowl until it holds a soft peak. Be careful not to overwhip and make the cream too stiff. Fold the whipped cream into the chilled raspberry mixture. Pour into a large, shallow pan and place in a very cold freezer. Freeze until half frozen, about 1½ hours, then remove. Scrape the sides and bottom of the pan and beat the mixture until it is smooth. Return to the freezer and freeze until firm, about 2 hours or more. Store at a normal freezer temperature.

GARY KETCHUM,
CREATIVE CULINARY SYSTEMS,
LITTLE ROCK, AR

Above: the City National Bank building in Fort Smith.

STRAWBERRY
SHORTCAKE

Strawberry shortcake is a sure sign of summer, certain to bring back happy memories.

PREPARATION TIME: 45 minutes
COOKING TIME: 20 minutes
YIELD: 1 large cake

INGREDIENTS

□ 2 cups flour   □ 3 tsps baking powder
□ 1 tbsp sugar   □ ¼ tsp salt
□ ½ cup shortening   □ ⅔ cup milk
□ 1 egg, beaten

TOPPING

□ ½ cup heavy cream   □ 1 tsp confectioners' sugar
□ ½ tsp vanilla   □ 1 quart fresh strawberries
□ ¼ cup sugar

To mix the shortcake, sift together the dry ingredients, then cut in the shortening. Stir in the milk and eggs. Knead the dough lightly and divide into two parts. Shape to fill a well greased 9-inch round baking tin. Bake at 425°F for 20 minutes. Set aside the cake to cool while you prepare the topping. To make the topping, whip the cream and fold in the vanilla and confectioners' sugar. Set aside 5 large, well-shaped strawberries to decorate the top of the shortcake. Crush the remaining berries with the granulated sugar.

To assemble the shortcake, cut the layer in half. Spread half of the crushed strawberries on the lower half. Top with half of the whipped cream and place the upper half of the cake on top. Decorate the top of the shortcake with the reserved strawberries.

GARY KETCHUM,
CREATIVE CULINARY SYSTEMS,
LITTLE ROCK, AR

Facing page: Banana Pudding.

BANANA PUDDING

This rich and creamy banana pudding is easily made and will be very much enjoyed.

PREPARATION TIME: 10 minutes

COOKING TIME: 15 minutes

SERVES: 4

INGREDIENTS

☐ 2 bananas, sliced ☐ ½ cup sugar
☐ 3 tbsps cornstarch ☐ ¼ tsp salt
☐ 1 pint milk ☐ 1 tsp vanilla
☐ 1 tsp butter

Heat the milk and add the sliced bananas. Sift together the sugar, cornstarch and salt. Stir in some of the hot milk to make a smooth paste, then stir the paste into the rest of the milk. Cook over a low heat, stirring constantly until thickened. Finally, blend in the vanilla and butter. Pour into 4 dessert glasses and chill before serving.

GARY KETCHUM,
CREATIVE CULINARY SYSTEMS,
LITTLE ROCK, AR

STAINED GLASS WINDOWS

*These are a beautiful addition to a Christmas reception, and one of Liza's
most often requested holiday treats.*

PREPARATION TIME: 20 minutes
COOKING TIME: 5 minutes
YIELD: 2 logs

INGREDIENTS

- 12oz semi-sweet chocolate chips
- ½ cup butter or margarine
- 6oz colored marshmallows
- ½ cup finely chopped pecans
- 12oz shredded coconut

In the top of a double boiler, melt the chocolate drops. Allow to cool slightly, then stir
in the marshmallows and pecans. Form the mixture into two logs and roll in the coconut.
Refrigerate until firm. To serve, slice into ¼-inch-thick slices.

LIZA, GOVERNOR'S MANSION,
LITTLE ROCK, AR

Above: Stained Glass Windows. Facing page: the restored War Eagle Mill.